Fodor's P O C K E T first edition

aruba

By Karen W. Bressler and Elise Rosen

D1315157

fodor's travel publications
new york • toronto • london • sydney • auckland
www.fodors.com

contents

ON THE ROAD WITH FODOR'S

EVERY TRIP IS SIGNIFICANT. Acutely aware of that fact, we've pulled out all stops in preparing *Fodor's Pocket Aruba*. To guide you in putting together your Aruba experience, we've created multiday itineraries and regional tours. And to direct you to the places that are truly worth your time and money, we've rallied the endearingly picky know-it-alls we're pleased to call our writers. Having seen all corners of Aruba, they're real experts. If you knew them, you'd poll them for tips yourself.

New York–based **Karen W. Bressler** escaped the northeastern winter to interview local celebrities in Aruba and tour their beautiful island. After clubbing at Club E and dipping her toes in the calm waters of Baby Beach, she compiled this exciting new guidebook which she hopes will convey Aruba as "one happy island." Karen has written for *Condé Nast Traveler*, *Bride's*, *Bridal Guide*, *Elegant Bride*, and *Honeymoon* magazines and is the Caribbean correspondent for Condé Nast's on-line travel publication, www.concierge.com. She has also contributed to *Fodor's Brazil*, *Fodor's Caribbean*, and *Fodor's Israel*, and has published several books including *Workout on the Go*, *A Century of Lingerie*, *Yoga Baby*, and *D.I.Y. Beauty*.

Elise Rosen—who worked side by side with Karen Bressler—has been a reporter for the Associated Press in New York and Los Angeles and a news producer for Time Warner's cable station, NY1 News. She began her career at a weekly community newspaper in her native Brooklyn; since then, her articles have appeared in publications throughout the United States and as far away as Saudi Arabia. Elise also has been an editorial contributor to several books, including *Fodor's Caribbean*, *Fodor's Israel*, *Career Opportunities in Art*, and *America's Elite 1000*.

We'd like to thank everyone at the Aruba Hotel and Tourism Authority (AHATA); Antonio Leo and the Aruba Tourism Authority; and friendly Aruban, Ian Tromp. Thanks also go to Suzanne Bressler, Barry and Sheila Weintrob, and Rhonda Zeller for their research assistance.

Don't Forget to Write

Keeping a travel guide fresh and up to date is a big job. So we love your feedback—positive and negative—and follow up on all suggestions. Contact the Aruba editor at editors@fodors.com or c/o Fodor's, 280 Park Avenue, New York, New York 10017. And have a wonderful trip!

Karen Cure

Editorial Director

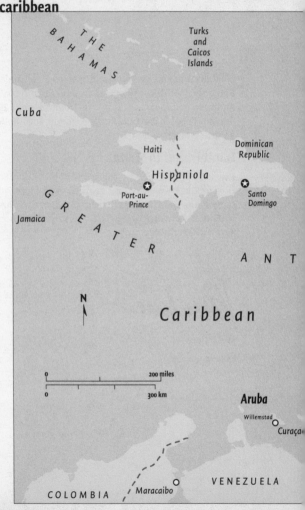

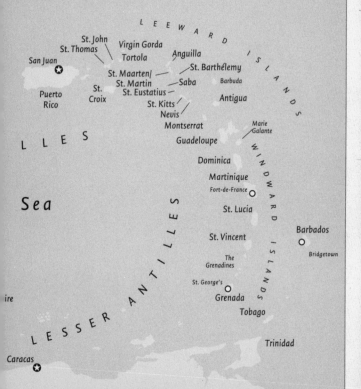

ATLANTIC OCEAN

LEEWARD ISLANDS

St. John
St. Thomas
Virgin Gorda
Tortola
San Juan
Anguilla
St. Barthélemy
St. Maarten/
St. Martin
Saba
Barbuda
Puerto
Rico
St.
Croix
St. Eustatius
Antigua
St. Kitts
Nevis
Montserrat
Marie
Galante
Guadeloupe
L L E S
WINDWARD ISLANDS
Dominica
Sea
Martinique
Fort-de-France
St. Lucia
Barbados
St. Vincent
Bridgetown
The
Grenadines
St. George's
Grenada
Tobago
ire
L E S S E R   A N T I L L E S
Trinidad
Caracas

aruba

The small crowd inside the main lounge of the cruise ship, which has just docked this morning, includes government officials and the press. They listen as the minister of tourism warmly greets the crew. Flashbulbs reflect off newly shined mirrors, and waiters pour champagne as the captain takes center stage. "I sailed to Aruba every week for almost 25 years, but that was a long time ago. I can't tell you how good it is to be back; now I know I'm home again."

In this Chapter

introducing aruba

FLAIR IS AN ARUBAN HALLMARK—flair for languages, music, food, hospitality, storytelling, and, above all, for life. You'll notice this joie de vivre as you meander through the streets or mingle with locals in a bar. Perhaps you'll revel in it as you paint the town red, dine at a fine restaurant, kick back at your hotel, or soak up the sun on a beach. Aruba's slogan sums it up best; this is, indeed, "One Happy Island."

The "A" in the ABC Islands (the other two being Bonaire and Curaçao), tiny Aruba got its name from the Arawak Indian word *oruba* (well placed), as it was convenient to South America. The conquistadors also found it a good jumping-off point for the Spanish Main, which held the promise of gold. They called the island *oro hubo*. There was gold, though gold wasn't found until many years after the conquistadors first arrived. Today both meanings hold true—Aruba is both a place of golden sunny days and a convenient vacation destination where golden memories are made.

Once a member of the Netherlands Antilles, the island became an independent entity within the Netherlands in 1986. Throughout its history Aruba's economy has relied on horse trading, gold (discovered here in 1824) mining, aloe vera cultivating, and refining Venezuelan oil. These days, however, tourism is the primary industry, and the island's population of 95,000 recognizes visitors as valued guests. The national anthem proclaims, "The greatness of our people is their great cordiality," and this is no exaggeration. Waiters serve you with smiles, English is spoken everywhere, and hotel hospitality directors appear delighted to fulfill your needs.

With its low humidity, average temperature of 28°C (82°F), modest rainfall, and location below the hurricane belt, Aruba seems like paradise. Silky sands and cooling trade winds have made the calm southwest coast a tourist mecca. Most of the island's 28 major hotels—with on-site restaurants, boutiques, and casinos—sit side by side down a single strip of shore. Every night sees theme parties, treasure hunts, beachside barbecues, or fish fries with steel bands and limbo or Carnival dancers. Surround all this with warm blue-green waters, and you've got the perfect destination for anyone who wants sun salted with lots of activities. Courteous service, efficient amenities, modern casinos, glorious beaches, duty-free shopping, and remarkably varied cuisine help fill Aruba's more than 7,500 hotel rooms.

THE MAKING OF ARUBA

THE PEOPLE

Aruba's first inhabitants were the Caiquetio Indians of the Arawak tribe (the earliest relics of their existence date from 2500 BC), who migrated from South America to avoid clashes with the more aggressive Caribs. The Arawaks formed a peaceful tribal society, living in small family groups, subsisting on fish, and making rudimentary tools from shells and stones. As their civilization developed, they turned to farming. Recent excavations in the Santa Cruz area have unearthed remnants of vessel pottery—cooking pots, baking griddles, burial urns, and other finely polished and painted pieces—and fragments of wooden house posts that indicate sophisticated design and manufacturing techniques. Indian inscriptions from about AD 1000 are still visible in Aruba's limestone caves.

Islandscapes

Set in the Caribbean Sea, Aruba is at latitude 12°30′ north and longitude 70° west and lies about 32 km (20 mi) from Venezuela's northern coast, near the Península Paraguaná. It's a small island, only 32 km (20 mi) long and 10 km (6 mi) across at its widest point, with a total area of 180 square km (70 square mi).

Aruba's topography is unusual for a Caribbean island. The southern and western coasts consist of miles of palm-lined, white-sand beaches. The calm, blue-green waters are so clear that in some areas visibility extends to a depth of 30 m (100 ft). The northeast coast is wild and rugged; here the waves pound against the coral cliffs, creating remarkable rock formations. The desert-like interior is home to various types of cactus and still more extraordinary rock formations. And everywhere, divi-divi trees flourish.

In the east, Arikok National Park makes up 18% of the island's total area. In the park is the 188-m (617-ft) Mt. Yamanota, Aruba's highest peak. The capital, Oranjestad, is on the southwest coast. Here Dutch and Spanish influences are evident in the colorful houses along Wilhelminastraat. Two main thoroughfares—J. E. Irausquin and L. G. Smith boulevards—link the capital to the hotels along Eagle and Palm beaches.

To the southeast lies San Nicolas, the island's second largest metropolis and the site of an oil refinery. At Aruba's northwestern tip are large rolling sand dunes as well as the island's newest golf course. Nestled at the island's heart, Santa Cruz is the cradle of religious culture, symbolized by a large cross marking the spot where Spanish missionaries introduced Christianity.

In about 1499 Spanish explorer Alonso de Ojeda (a lieutenant of Christopher Columbus's) was the first European to land on the island. According to oral history, an Arawak chieftain guided the first Spanish arrivals inland, where they erected a cross to mark the occasion. (In 1968 this event was commemorated by the placement of a large wooden cross atop a rocky hill in Santa Cruz.) Believing there were no precious metals—alluvial gold wasn't found until 1824—in 1515 the conquerors exported the entire Indian population to Hispaniola (today's Dominican Republic and Haiti) to work in the copper mines there. Though some Indians were allowed to return after 1527, when Spain began actively to colonize Aruba, Bonaire, and Curaçao, the mass abduction ended much of the Arawak culture on the island.

In 1636, during the Eighty Years' War between Holland and Spain, the Dutch took control of Aruba, Bonaire, and Curaçao, ruling them under the charter of the Dutch West India Company. Over the next 100 years, commerce grew on the island, which served as a satellite to the administrative center on larger Curaçao.

Owing to the arid climate and poor soil, Aruba was spared from plantation economics and the slave trade; instead, the Dutch used the remaining Arawaks to herd cattle. The Dutch held power until 1805, when the English laid claim to Aruba briefly during the Napoleonic Wars. The Dutch Republic on the European continent had fallen to the French in 1795, and France annexed the Netherlands in 1810. But after Napoléon's defeat in 1815, political lines throughout Europe were redrawn. The Kingdom of the Netherlands was born, and in 1816 possession of Aruba was returned permanently to the Dutch.

In 1750, Domingo Antonio Silvestre—who had been converted to Catholicism by Spanish missionaries—built a small chapel at Alto Vista on the island's north shore to accommodate the Catholic community, which until this time had had no formal place of worship. The winding approach road is lined with 12 white crosses indicating the stations of the cross, which pilgrims can follow to the tranquil chapel. The Santa Anna Church, built in the district of Noord in 1776, is renowned for its handsomely carved oak altar, which was awarded a prize for neo-Gothic design at the Rome exhibition of 1870.

The first Protestant church was built in 1848 in the center of Oranjestad. The original building houses a Bible museum and is maintained by the congregation; an adjoining larger church is used for weekly services. Another landmark house of worship, the Immaculada Concepción Church in Santa Cruz, is noted for the colorful biblical mural decorating its nave. The Beth Israel Synagogue was built in 1962 to meet the needs of the growing Jewish community. (Its members originally arrived in the 1920s, when an international workforce was drawn to Aruba to staff the oil refinery.)

With a history full of cultures clashing and melding, it's no surprise that most islanders are fluent in several languages. School lessons are taught in Dutch, the official language. Arubans begin studying English, recognized as the international tongue, as early as the fourth grade. Spanish, essential due to Aruba's proximity to South America, is taught in school as early as fifth grade, and French is offered as an option in high school. In normal conversation, however, the locals speak Papiamento —a mix of Spanish, Dutch, Portuguese, English, and French, as well as Indian and African languages. Since 1998, Papiamento has also been taught in grade school (☞ portrait and box, *below*).

THE ECONOMY

Early on, Aruba's main source of income was drawn from exporting horses—brought in by the Spanish and bred on the island—to Jamaica and Cuba. In the 16th century, Aruba was a free-roaming horse ranch. There were no European settlements other than garrisons until the 19th century. Later, the island's

Arawak population herded cattle that was traded or sold to Curaçao and made glass objects to sell. The first white colonists arrived from Curaçao in 1754, and several merchant families followed. There were few opportunities for income on the island before gold was found. Many who settled here in the 18th century worked in Venezuela as seasonal laborers on coffee and cocoa plantations; others headed for Jamaica and Cuba. Then in 1824 the discovery of gold on the island's northern slopes at Rooi Fluit boosted the economy. Intermittent reports of gold finds led several exploration companies to set up shop, until the gold was exhausted and the related businesses ceased operations in 1916.

Another major revenue source was the cultivation of aloe (raw sap from the plant was used as a laxative). By the 1920s Aruba was responsible for 70% of the world's aloe supply, with England accounting for most of the intake. The crop brought in about $1 million per year. Calcium phosphate was also a source of income for a while; it was mined in Aruba from 1879 to 1914 and exported to Europe and the United States.

But it was oil that ultimately fueled Aruba's economic boom. In 1924, the Lago refinery was built in San Nicolas. Searching for a hospitable seaport and a stable political climate in which to process the oil from Venezuela's Lake Maracaibo fields, the Standard Oil Company of New Jersey (later Exxon) took over the refinery in 1932. It was soon producing 440,000 barrels of refined oil a day. The company hired thousands of North Americans, Arubans, and other Caribbean islanders, and San Nicolas thrived as residential and commercial areas sprang up to accommodate the workforce.

The refinery played an integral role in World War II, producing one in every 16 gallons of motor fuel used by the Allies. A German submarine had orders to destroy the refinery in 1942 but was unable to fire its cannons. Historians theorize that this failure was one of the events that tipped the hand of victory toward the Allies. By 1949 the refinery had 8,300 employees—

roughly 16% of the populace. Indeed, Aruba's population grew sixfold in the three decades after the refinery was built, surging from 9,000 in 1924 to 54,000 in 1954.

Due to an unstable oil market, however, the refinery was closed in 1985. Although the Coastal Corporation of Texas reopened it in 1991 (and it now produces 150,000 barrels a day), the tourist trade has replaced oil as Aruba's primary source of income. Education, health care, and other public services are financed by tourism, which has also helped to keep the unemployment rate at less than 1%. For these reasons, it's no surprise that guests are warmly received. This warmth has, in turn, contributed to an increase in visitors—from 206,750 in 1985 to 683,300 in 1999.

THE GOVERNMENT

Until late 1985 Aruba was a member of the Netherlands Antilles, along with Bonaire, Curaçao, St. Maarten, St. Eustatius, and Saba. On January 1, 1986 Aruba was granted a new status as an independent entity within the Kingdom of the Netherlands, which now consists of the Netherlands, the Netherlands Antilles, and Aruba.

The island has a royally appointed governor, who acts as the Dutch sovereign's representative for a six-year term. Executive power is held by the seven-member council of ministers, appointed by the legislative council for four-year terms and presided over by the prime minister, who is elected every four years. The legislature consists of a parliament whose 21 members are elected by popular vote to serve a four-year term. Legal jurisdiction lies with the Common Court of Justice of Aruba and the Netherlands Antilles as well as the Supreme Court of Justice at the Hague in the Netherlands. Defense and foreign affairs still fall under the realm of the kingdom, while internal matters involving such things as customs, immigration, aviation, and communications are handled autonomously.

Betico Croes (1938–85)

Arubans are proud of their autonomous standing within the Kingdom of the Netherlands, and it's Gilberto François "Betico" Croes who is heralded as the hero behind the island's status aparte (separate status). His birthday, January 25, is an official Aruban holiday.

During the Dutch colonial expansion of the 17th century, Aruba and five other islands—Bonaire, Curaçao, St. Maarten, St. Eustatius, and Saba—became territories known as the Netherlands Antilles. After World War II, these islands began to pressure Holland for autonomy, and in 1954, they became a collective self-governing entity under the umbrella of the Kingdom of the Netherlands.

At this time, there were several political parties in power on the island. Soon, however, Juancho Irausquin (who has a major thoroughfare named in his honor) formed a new party that maintained control for nearly two decades. Irausquin was considered the founder of Aruba's new economic order and the forebear of modern Aruban politics. After his death, his party's power diminished.

In 1971 Croes, then a young, ambitious school administrator, became the leader of another political party. Bolstered by a thriving economy generated by Aruba's oil refinery, Croes spearheaded the island's cause to secede from the Netherlands Antilles and to gain status as an equal partner within the Dutch kingdom. Sadly, he didn't live to celebrate the realization of his dream. On December 31, 1985, the day before Aruba's new status became official, Croes was in a car accident that put him in a coma for 11 months. He died on November 26, 1986. Etched in the minds of Arubans are his prophetic words: "Si mi cai na cominda, gara e bandera y sigui cu e lucha" ("If I die along the way, seize the flag and go on with the struggle").

PORTRAITS

ONE LANGUAGE FOR ALL

Papiamento is a unique Creole language—a mellifluous blend of African, European, and Arawak Indian tongues—that's widely spoken on Aruba, Bonaire, and Curaçao. One theory holds that Papiamento originated on Curaçao in the 17th century to afford a means of communication between African slaves and their Dutch owners. Another holds that the language developed somewhat earlier, blending the tongues of the Spanish settlers and the indigenous population. In either case, over time, words were incorporated from still other peoples, including Portuguese and Spanish missionaries and South American traders. Still later, it was peppered with some English and French elements.

Linguists believe the name Papiamento (a variation of Papiamentu) probably derives from the Portuguese verb *papiar*, meaning "to chatter." In Papiamento, as in some other Creole languages, the verb *papia* means "to speak." Add the suffix *mentu*, which in Papiamento means "the way of doing something" and you form a noun. Thus, Papiamento is roughly translated as "the way of speaking." (Sometimes the suffix *-mentu* is spelled in the Spanish and Portuguese way [*-mento*], creating the variant spelling.)

Papiamento began as an oral tradition, handed down through the generations and spoken by all social classes. On Aruba, you'll hear a melodic, lilting tone to the language; on Curaçao, the delivery is more rapid-fire; and in Bonaire, the sound is somewhere in between. There's no uniform spelling or grammar from island to island or even from one neighborhood to another on the same island.

In 1995 Aruba's citizens began a grassroots effort to raise awareness of Papiamento and to have it taught in the schools. It was made part of the curriculum in 1998; that year was also declared the Year of Papiamento on Aruba. With its official recognition, Papiamento continues to be refined and standardized.

INTERVIEW WITH ARUBA'S MINISTER OF ECONOMIC AFFAIRS AND TOURISM

Admired throughout the island, Lilia Genara Beke-Martinez, M.D. isn't a government official to mess with. As the minister of economic affairs, she's responsible for the country's economic, social, and cultural well-being. As the minister of tourism, she's responsible for the growth of the tourism industry. Under her leadership, airline service to the island has increased, pensions have doubled, and welfare payments have been raised substantially. She has reinstated several local cultural events and helped to reorganize historic preservation programs. For this minister, it's all in a day's work.

FODOR'S TRAVEL GUIDES (FTG): How has the tourism industry changed over the past 10 years?

BEKE-MARTINEZ (BM): Worldwide, the trend of tourism has drastically changed. Tourists travel far and are looking for new horizons. In a nutshell tourism has been modernized in every aspect. The tourist of this century is looking for sophisticated, adventurous, and exciting vacations.

FTG: What are the main reasons people visit Aruba?

BM: Aruban people are friendly, and hospitality is an inborn asset. And the fact that Aruba is outside the hurricane belt doesn't hurt either. Aruba's beaches are spectacular, and the hotels range from first to middle class with a wide choice for everyone. Our island is small but very interesting . . . our history can be traced back for 4,000 years.

FTG: Do visitors ever impose on the lifestyle of the Aruban people?

Papiamento Primer

Arubans enjoy it when visitors use their language, so don't be shy. You can buy a Papiamento dictionary to build your vocabulary, but here are a few pleasantries—terms of friendship and love—to get you started:

Bon dia.	Good morning.
Bon tardi.	Good afternoon.
Bon nochi.	Good evening/night.
Bon bini.	Welcome.
Ajo.	Bye.
Te aworo.	See you later.
Pasa un bon dia.	Have a good day.
Danki.	Thank you.
Na bo ordo.	You're welcome.
Con ta bai?	How are you?
Mi ta bon.	I am fine.
Ban goza!	Let's enjoy!
Pabien!	Congratulations!
Hopi bon	Very good
Ami	Me
Abo	You
Nos dos	The two of us
Mi dushi	My sweetheart
Ku tur mi amor	With all my love
Un sunchi	A kiss
Un braza	A hug
Ranka lenga	To French kiss
Mi stima Aruba.	I love Aruba.

BM: [There is a] certain influence due to the influx of tourists. . . . However, due to the already mentioned hospitality of the Aruban people and their knowledge of several languages, this influence is not a setback. . . .

FTG: Do you have a story of a special encounter with a tourist or of a tourist who has touched your life?

BM: While having dinner with my family in a well-known restaurant, we started a conversation with a couple who were on vacation. It turned out that they had been coming to Aruba for the last 15 years and that the first and most exciting thing for them to do whenever they arrived at their hotel was to drink the water straight out of the tap. That really made me feel good.

FTG: Where do you go on vacation and why?

BM: In my function, vacation is something that comes along once in a while and is always very short; I would say one week a year for the past six years. This year, though, I do plan to take a seven-day cruise.

FTG: Do you avoid tourist-oriented restaurants or other establishments? What's your favorite local hangout?

BM: Due to the size of Aruba, it is very difficult to avoid places, and they [all] can get crowded. My favorite hangout is my home.

FTG: What's the most exciting part of your job? What's the most challenging part of your job?

BM: The most exciting part of my job is to be able to accomplish something for our people. The most challenging part is to convince everybody that we've accomplished something.

FTG: What are you most proud of about your island?

BM: I am proud of our people; they are the ones who carry the island.

FTG: What's special about the Aruban people?

BM: Their hospitality, friendliness, and their love of life itself.

FTG: What changes do you hope to see in Aruba in the next 10 years?

BM: Honestly, I do hope that the people of Aruba will not change; I hope that they stay the way they are.

ISLANDERS

Since Aruba gained its status aparte, many of its people have worked hard to develop the local economy, particularly tourism. This has sometimes meant letting the lines between Aruban culture and the cultures of its visitors blur. Yet one characteristic still flourishes among Arubans—their desire to help others. What follows are two profiles of Arubans who are known for their kindness to others and for their dedication to their people.

A Cabbie's Road to Friendship

Janchi Hart, a local taxi driver, was once approached by an American cruise-ship passenger who needed a ride to the hospital to visit her husband, who had broken his ankle in an island mall. As a result of Hart's friendly, accommodating manner, the visitor hired him to take her around the island throughout her stay. After she and her husband returned home, Hart called the couple to see how they had managed in their travels. They were so touched by this gesture that they began a correspondence and have since visited him and his family in Aruba.

As a result of his extra efforts, Hart won an award from the Aruba Quality Foundation and was asked to represent the island at a dinner celebrating friendship in Chicago on New Year's Eve, 1999. He and his wife joined tourism representatives from all over the world in festivities complete with fireworks and a city tour.

Hart continues to drive his taxi and remains unfazed by such typical tourist questions as "How's the weather?" and "How many miles is it to the hotel?" He says he likes his job because he meets different kinds of people every day, but he could do without the traffic caused by the island's 400 cabs. Still, with so many taxis, it's no wonder that Hart and his compatriots are always at your service.

Beauty Works

Tamara Scaroni held the title of Miss Aruba from July 1999 to July 2000. Scaroni, who followed in the footsteps of her mother (Miss Aruba 1969), originally entered the beauty pageant to win prize money for a college degree in international business. But her involvement in the competition led to much more. As Miss Aruba, she served as a United Nations AIDS Ambassador, lecturing at schools about the disease and preventative measures, organizing a talk show to increase AIDS awareness on Aruba, and creating a local TV commercial about a patient living with the illness. In addition, she helped to plan a fashion show that raised money for a hospital dedicated to children with disabilities.

The beauty queen hopes that, by example, she taught Aruban women about being the best they could be instead of changing to meet the expectations of others. Although she dons designer dresses for pageants, simple clothes—comfortable jeans and casual dresses—define her everyday style. She normally wears only a little mascara and some lipstick, rather than the tons of foundation and powder she donned for TV spots and personal appearances. True to her low-key style, her biggest surprise during her tenure as Miss Aruba was that people actually wanted her autograph.

Scaroni plans to start a consultancy that will help local companies stay in business. She also plans to continue promoting Aruba in every way possible and, perhaps, launch her own political career. Then it may well be back to the personal appearances, heavy makeup, and autographs.

Distance Conversion Chart

Kilometers/Miles

To change kilometers (km) to miles (mi), multiply km by .621.
To change mi to km, multiply mi by 1.61.

km to mi	mi to km
1 = .62	1 = 1.6
2 = 1.2	2 = 3.2
3 = 1.9	3 = 4.8
4 = 2.5	4 = 6.4
5 = 3.1	5 = 8.1
6 = 3.7	6 = 9.7
7 = 4.3	7 = 11.3
8 = 5.0	8 = 12.9

Meters/Feet

To change meters (m) to feet (ft), multiply m by 3.28.
To change ft to m, multiply ft by .305.

m to ft	ft to m
1 = 3.3	1 = .30
2 = 6.6	2 = .61
3 = 9.8	3 = .92
4 = 13.1	4 = 1.2
5 = 16.4	5 = 1.5
6 = 19.7	6 = 1.8
7 = 23.0	7 = 2.1
8 = 26.2	8 = 2.4

A tiny, yellow-bellied barika geel lands on the table and glares enviously at the buffet breakfast of muffins, mangoes, and berries. The waves glisten in the background and the sun lights up his colorful feathers as he flutters impatiently and staggers around, trying to plan his next move. Even the seagulls gliding overhead can't divert his attention. Someone puts a morsel of food in front of him; he eagerly grabs it before flying off into the warm air of another perfect Aruban day.

In this Chapter

perfect days and nights

ARE YOU PERPLEXED ABOUT WHICH OF ARUBA'S MANY BEACHES is best or about how to spend your time during one of the island's rare rainy days? Below are some suggestions to guide you. There are also a few ideas on how to spend a night (or two) celebrating all the perfect days you've been having.

A PERFECT DAY AT THE BEACH

Aruba's white sands and turquoise waters are legendary, but for perfection, head to the island's southernmost tip, where the beaches are the most secluded. Just make sure you wear plenty of sunscreen; the cooling trade winds can be deceiving.

Before setting out, rent snorkel gear at your hotel so that you can fully appreciate the calm water and all its inhabitants. And why not pack a picnic? Many hotels will prepare one at your request, or you can stop by a supermarket (there are several on L. G. Smith Boulevard) to pick up provisions for the day.

The Kadushi Juice Bar at the foot of the beachfront pool area at the Hyatt Regency Aruba (☞ Where to Sleep) is a great place to start your day. Slowly sip a fruit or veggie smoothie as you relax on a lounge chair overlooking the waves. From here, make the

27-km (17-mi) trip by rental car southeast to Baby Beach, which is as placid as a wading pool and just about as shallow (only 4–5 ft deep). The shady, thatched areas that dot its sands are ideal for cooling off.

Splash about in the water and do a little snorkeling. Try your hand at a game of paddleball or Frisbee (buy or rent equipment before setting out). In the afternoon, sack out on the sand and get some well-deserved rest. After all, you're on vacation. Be sure to wake up in time for happy hour (it starts at 5 PM) at Rodger's Beach Snack Bar, an eight-minute walk northwest of Baby Beach. There's often live entertainment here; regardless, it's a great place to grab a rum punch and chill.

A PERFECT RAINY DAY

Aruba has a reputation for guaranteed sunshine because of its location outside the hurricane belt. But weather patterns can be unpredictable. Here's what to do if you get caught in a storm.

Have breakfast at DeliFrance (☞ Eating Out) in the Certified Mega Mall on L. G. Smith Boulevard. The freshly baked bagels and the hot Dutch pancakes covered in powdered sugar will surely warm you up. By 10 or so, head to downtown Oranjestad's Archaeological Museum (☞ Here and There), where you'll find a vast collection of Indian artifacts, farm and domestic utensils, and skeletons. Spend an hour walking around, and you'll get a taste of Aruban history. Another option is the Eagle Bowling Palace (☞ Outdoor Activities and Sports), which has 16 lanes, a cocktail lounge, and a snack bar. You'll never know how frightful the weather is outside.

For lunch, head to the pool bar at the Divi Aruba Beach Resort (☞ Where to Sleep), where the brick oven cooks up the island's tastiest pizzas. Make-your-own-daiquiri machines wait for you to fulfill your bartending fantasies. The canopy over the bar will shield you from the rain, and the people on the bar stools beside you will no doubt swap stories with you (and maybe even drinks) or start singing songs.

After lunch, treat yourself to a massage. Try the Claudine Beauty Clinic at the Aruba Marriott Resort and Stellaris Casino (☞ Where to Sleep), which offers Swedish, sports-reflexology, and aromatherapy massages (55 minutes, $99; 30 minutes, $60). Your body will thank you. Your soul will, too. Stick around to shop, gamble, or just relax for a few hours. You might also want to hop in a cab and head for the airport to extend your airline ticket (in hopes of a few more sunny days). Wrap up your rainy day with a 7:30 movie at the Seaport Cinema in the Seaport Village Market Place. Its six theaters show the latest American movies in English.

A PERFECT NIGHT OF ROMANCE

When the sun goes down, Aruba becomes one of the most romantic settings on earth. Here's how to share it with that special someone.

Make reservations at Brisas Del Mar (☞ Eating Out), which is always packed at sunset. Ask for a table on the terrace, where the breeze is inviting and the ocean view is mesmerizing. If you're lucky, the long-time owner will join you for a bit and tell wonderful stories of past guests. Be careful what you say—you will be one some day.

Have dinner at Le Dôme (☞ Eating Out), another place where reservations are required. Service doesn't get any better than this; neither does food. Share a delectable French dish, dive into a dessert for two, order some coffee, and cozy up on the couch in the center of the main dining room.

After dinner, head for the Sirocco Lounge in the Wyndham's Casablanca Casino (☞ Casinos). Sip a cocktail and listen to live jazz (every night but Wednesday and Sunday). Or be daring and puff on an authentic Arabian hookah pipe. Later, pick a random number on the roulette wheel at the Sonesta's Crystal Casino (☞ Casinos). If it's not a winner, try numbers that have special meaning for you, like each other's birthday, your wedding anniversary, or the day you met. End the evening with a walk—hand in hand of course—along the beach.

A PERFECT ALL-NIGHTER

Want to take advantage of everything Aruba has to offer? Here's an action-packed guide of things to do from sundown to sun-up.

Check out the Sunset Salute, accompanied by live music, at the Radisson Sunset Bar in the Radisson Aruba Caribbean Resort (☞ Where to Sleep). Stick around for drink specials and merengue lessons.

Make dinner reservations at L'Escale (☞ Eating Out), an upscale eatery overlooking the marina at the Aruba Sonesta Resort. You'll be serenaded by a Hungarian string trio as the courteous staff caters to your every need. The succulent dishes—fresh mahimahi, Caribbean-style snapper, rich chocolate soufflé—will surely satisfy your appetite.

At 9 PM, check out *Hot Tickets*—an entertaining, international revue of singing and dancing—at the Sonesta Hotel's Stardust Theatre (☞ Casinos). Afterward, head to the trendy Garufa (☞ Nightlife) lounge for live jazz, a cognac, and perhaps a stogie. The chic bar stools are so comfortable, you may not want to leave for a good long while. And besides, the later you get to the Club E (☞ Nightlife) for dancing, the more fun you'll have. Known for wild parties in its VIP room and for its eclectic collection of music (played 'til the wee hours), this is one place not to miss on your all-night adventure.

By sunrise, you should be on the beach—any beach. It just doesn't get any better than this. Afterward sip coffee, scan the local papers, and people-watch over breakfast at the Coco Plum café (☞ Eating Out). Carbo-load for the new day with a *pastechi*—a potato-filled pastry.

The restaurant, typically packed with tourists, is now full of locals on an afternoon outing. They're joined at the bar by a visitor from New York who has befriended them to learn more about island life. After a few Balashi beers, the stories flow—tales of "yesterday's soup" (a belief that soup tastes better the second day) and jouvert (a street party that starts at 3 AM and lasts 'til sunrise to kick off Carnival). When their table is ready, the Arubans invite their new friend along to sample native specialties. The New Yorker hadn't planned to dine on goat stew, but when in Rome....

In this Chapter

eating out

THERE ARE A FEW HUNDRED RESTAURANTS ON ARUBA, including hotel establishments, neighborhood eateries, snack bars, and fast-food chains, so you're bound to find something to tantalize your taste buds. Thanks to the island's eclectic blend of cultures, local eateries serve the full gamut from Aruban food to American, Italian, French, Argentine, Asian, and Cuban. Chefs have to be creative here, since there's a limited number of locally grown ingredients—*maripampoen* (a vegetable that's often stewed with meat and potatoes), *hierba di hole* (a sweet-spicy herb used in fish soup), and *shimarucu* (a fruit similar to a cherry) are among the few.

Although most resorts offer better-than-average dining, don't be afraid to try one of the many excellent, reasonably priced, independent places. Ask locals about their favorite spots; some of the lesser-known restaurants offer food that's definitely worth sampling.

Most restaurants are along Palm Beach or in Oranjestad, easily accessible by taxi or the buses that run regularly to and from town. Some restaurants in San Nicolas are worth the trip; renting a car is the best way to get there.

To give visitors a chance to sample the island's eclectic cuisine, the **Aruba Gastronomic Association** (AGA; Rooi Santo 21, Noord, tel. 297/8–62161 or 800/477–2896 in the U.S., www. arubadining.com) has created a dine-around program involving several island restaurants. Here's how it works: you can buy tickets for 3 dinners ($109 per person), 5 dinners ($177), 7 dinners ($245), or 10 dinners ($339). Dinners include an appetizer, an entrée, dessert, coffee or tea, and service charge (where applicable). Other programs, such as multicourse VIP gourmet dinners and after-dinner-show packages, are also available. You can buy dine-around tickets on the AGA's Web site (using an on-line-fax order form), through travel agents, or at the De Palm Tours sales desk in your hotel.

Prices and Dress

Aruba's elegant restaurants—where you might have to dress up a little (jackets for men, sundresses for women)—can be pricey. If you want to spend fewer florins, opt for the more casual spots, where being comfortable is the only dress requirement. A sweater draped over your shoulders will go a long way against the chill of air-conditioning. If you plan to eat in the open air, bring along insect repellent in case the mosquitoes get unruly.

CATEGORY	COST*
$$$	over $25
$$	$15–$25
$	under $15

*per person for a three-course meal, excluding drinks, 10%–15% service charge, and tax

How and When

To ensure you get to eat at the restaurants of your choice, make some calls when you get to the island—especially during high season—to secure reservations. If you're heading to a restaurant in Oranjestad for dinner, leave about 15 minutes earlier than you think you should; in-town traffic can become ugly once beach hours are over. Note that on Sunday, you may have a hard time finding a restaurant outside of a hotel that's open for lunch, and many restaurants are closed for dinner on Sunday or Monday. Breakfast lovers are in luck. For quantity, check out the buffets at

Chowing Aruban Style

The finest restaurants require at the most only a jacket for men and a sundress for women. Still, after a day on the beach, even this might feel formal. For a truly casual bite, visit one of Aruba's ice cream trucks or frietjes (pushcarts) for inexpensive, authentic Aruban finger food. Two worth the trip are El Rey Snack Truck near the Seaport Cinemas in Oranjestad, for freshly fried chicken, pork chops, and fries, and The Cellar Frietje in Oranjestad's Seaport Village Marketplace, for the best saté in town. Other island delicacies include the following:

Bitterballen: steaming, bite-size meatballs. The long versions are served with mustard and called kroket. Locals wash both varieties down with beer.

Frekedel: shredded fish dipped in egg and bread crumbs, rolled into balls, and deep fried.

Friet or Batata: french fries—served in paper cones or Styrofoam cups— that can be topped with ketchup; mayo; curry, peanut, or hot sauce; onions; and more.

Keshi Yena: a baked concoction of Gouda cheese, spices, and meat or seafood in a rich brown sauce.

Nasibal: a lump of seasoned rice in a crunchy coating.

Pan Bati: a pancake made of cornmeal flour, sugar, salt, and baking powder; eaten with meat, fish, or soup.

Pastechi: deep-fried meat, cheese, potato, or seafood-filled turnovers, popular for breakfast. Smaller versions are called empanas.

Raspao: a paper cup full of shaved ice that's drenched in fruit-flavored (tamarind, guava, passion fruit) syrup.

Roti: chicken, seafood, or vegetable curry in a tortilla-like wrap.

Saté: marinated chunks of chicken or pork on a bamboo skewer, grilled and served with spicy peanut sauce.

Tosti: the ultimate grilled-cheese sandwich, often made with ham and pineapple or pepperoni.

the Hyatt, Marriott, or Wyndham resorts (☞ Where to Sleep) or local joints like DeliFrance or Coco Plum (☞ below).

ARGENTINE

$$ **EL GAUCHO ARGENTINE GRILL.** Faux-leather-bound books, tulip-top lamps, wooden chairs, and tile floors decorate this Argentine steak house, which has been in business for more than 20 years. A bottle of rich red wine from the extensive cellar and the melt-in-your-mouth garlic bread will tantalize your taste buds as you await your meal. Main dishes include thick *churrasco* (Argentine steak) smothered in peppers and onions and served with corn on the cob, potatoes, and broccoli or the catch of the day (perhaps, grouper) served with salad, rice, broccoli, and fried plantains. For dessert, go for the *helado Argentino* (vanilla ice cream with sweet-potato marmalade and caramel) or the *torta de queso*, otherwise known as cheesecake. *Wilhelminastraat 80, Oranjestad, tel. 297/8–23677. AE, D, MC, V. Closed Sun.*

ASIAN

$$–$$$ **JAKARTA.** Brightly painted stone walls, fringed lamp shades, colorful paintings, and clusters of candles bring this restaurant to life. The signature rijsttafel will jump off the page of the straw-faced, banana-leaf-covered menu. It consists of 20 miniature meat, fish, vegetable, and fruit dishes; the Indonesian spices can bring tears to your eyes. Another popular choice is Indonesian-style chicken soup, made with bean sprouts, hard-boiled eggs, and chicken liver. Vegetarians can order egg rolls, vegetable soup, or a veggie rijsttafel. If the air-conditioning is too strong indoors, sit on the back patio, decked with a bamboo bar, wind chimes, big clay pots, and tiki torches (if the bugs start to bite, ask for a mosquito-repelling candle). Try an exotic drink with your meal; good choices include java juice (blue Curaçao, vodka, Cointreau, banana liqueur, and orange and pineapple juice), a mai tai, or a scorpion. *Wilhelminastraat 64, Oranjestad, tel. 297/8–38737. AE, D, DC, MC, V. Closed Tues.*

$–$$ KOWLOON. In addition to many Chinese provinces, Indonesia is also represented on the menu here. Try the *bami goreng*, a noodle dish with shreds of shrimp, pork, vegetables, and an Indonesian blend of herbs and spices. *Saté* (grilled strips of beef or chicken in a spicy peanut sauce), curried dishes, and steak prepared in a variety of ways are also available. The modern Asian decor blends well with the island's palms and sands. *Emmastraat 1, Oranjestad, tel. 297/8–24950. AE, MC, V.*

CAFÉ

$ THE INTERNET CAFÉ. Vacations are great, but sometimes you still need contact with the outside world. Instead of toting your laptop through customs, click on at some of the recently installed kiosks in the lobbies of the Marriott, Hyatt, and Tamarijn hotels (☞ Where to Sleep). Or come to this cybercafé, where you can sip coffee as you surf ($3 for 15 minutes, $6 for 30 minutes). Order some coffee and cake or cookies, grab some candy from the candy machine, and pick up a souvenir T-shirt on your way out. *Royal Plaza Mall, L. G. Smith Blvd. 204, Oranjestad, tel. 297/8–24500. D, DC, MC, V.*

CARIBBEAN

$$–$$$ BOONOONOONOOS. The name—say it just as it looks— means "extraordinary" in Papiamento, a bit of hyperbole for this Caribbean bistro in the heart of Oranjestad. The decor is festive with fiesta colors, ceramic lamps, and palm thatching. The specialty is Pan-Caribbean cuisine, and the dishes are accompanied by hearty portions of peas, rice, and plantains. The Jamaican jerk ribs (a 300-year-old recipe) are tiny but spicy; the roast chicken Barbados (topped with plantain and coconut) and the pumpkin soup are also good choices. You may want to

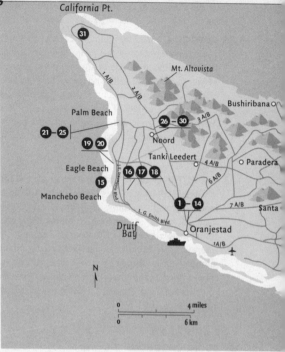

California Pt.

31

Mt. Altovista

1 A/B

2 A/B

Bushiribana

Palm Beach

26 — 30

3 A/B

Noord

21 — 25

Tanki Leedert

19 20

Eagle Beach

16 17 18

Paradera

L. G. Smith Blvd.

4 A/B

15

Manchebo Beach

6 A/B

7 A/B

1 14

Santa

L. G. Smith Blvd.

Druif
Bay

Oranjestad

1 A/B

N

0   4 miles

0   6 km

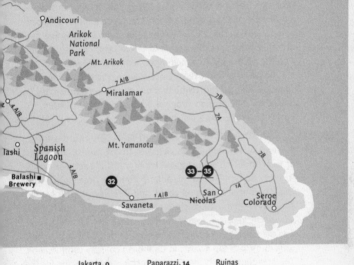

KEY

🚢 cruise ship terminal

① restaurants

stop by for lunch, when prices average about $8 per person. (Note that this restaurant is part of the AGA's dine-around program.) *Wilhelminastraat 18A, Oranjestad, tel. 297/8–31888. AE, DC, MC, V. No lunch Sun.*

$$–$$$ DRIFTWOOD. The charming co-owner, Francine Merryweather, greets you at the door of this Aruban restaurant, which is tastefully decorated to look like a series of fishermen's huts. Order the fish of the day prepared as you like it (Aruban style— pan-fried with a sauce of fresh tomato, green pepper, chopped onions, local herbs, and oil—is best) or another of the fine fish dishes. Of the specially prepared drinks, you can't go wrong with the white sangria punch; if you're nice to the maître d', he may let you take home the recipe. While you're at it, ask him for some casino tips, too. (Note that this restaurant participates in the AGA's dine-around program.) *Klipstraat 12, Oranjestad, tel. 297/8–32515. AE, MC, V. Closed Tues.*

$$–$$$ GASPARITO RESTAURANT AND ART GALLERY. This charming,
★ no-smoking restaurant is also a gallery that showcases the works of local artists on softly lighted white walls. It's set in a *cunucu* (country house)—in Noord, not far from the hotel strip—with lovely highback hardwood chairs and steel lamps. The Aruban specialties—pan bati, keshi yena, fish croquettes, conch stew, stewed chicken, creole-style fish fillet—are a feast for both the eye and the palate, so it comes as no surprise that Gasparito's chefs walk away with top awards in Caribbean culinary competitions. The standout dish is the Gasparito chicken; the recipe for the sauce comes from the owner's ancestors and features seven special ingredients including brandy, white wine, and pineapple juice (the rest are secret!). Service is excellent, and the restaurant participates in the AGA's dine-around program. *Gasparito 3, Noord, tel. 297/8–67044. AE, D, MC, V. Closed Sun. No lunch.*

$$–$$$ JOEY'S. Of all the island's Caribbean restaurants, Joey's comes closest to offering authentic Aruban dishes (*and it's part of the*

Some Like It Hot!

Arubans like it hot, and that's where the island's famous Madame Jeanette sauce comes in handy. It's made with chili peppers that are so hot they can burn your skin when they're broken open. Whether they're turned into pika, a relish-like mixture made with papaya, or sliced thin into vinegar and onions, these peppers are sure to set your mouth on fire. Throw even a modest amount of Madame Jeanette sauce into a huge pot of soup, and your taste buds will tingle. (As a word play on the sauce's spicy nature, Aruban men often refer to an attractive woman as a "Madame Jeanette.") To tame the flames, don't go for a glass of water, as capsaicin, the compound in peppers that lights the fire, isn't water-soluble. Yogurt, sweet fruits, and starchy foods such as rice and bread are the best remedies.

AGA's dine-around program). The food here is a far cry from what's served at your local fish-and-chips joint back home. If you have a daring palate, venture in for at least one dinner. Entrées include fresh local fish dishes, vegetable dishes (featuring such seasonal produce as okra or cucumber), and stewed conch or goat. *La Quinta Resort, Savaneta 121, Savaneta, tel. 297/8–45049. AE, D, DC, MC, V. No lunch. Closed Wed.*

$$–$$$ **OLD CUNUCU HOUSE RESTAURANT.** For more than seven years executive chef Ligia Maria has been delighting diners with delicious homemade meals, earning her a reputation as one of Aruba's finest chefs. Try the keshi yena or the Caribbean lobster tail, broiled and served with a thermidor cream sauce and topped with Parmesan cheese. For dessert, indulge in Spanish coffee with Tia Maria and brandy. Friday night sees musical entertainment; Saturday night features a mariachi band and all the chicken and beef fajitas you can eat. (Note that this restaurant participates in the AGA's dine-around program.) *Palm Beach 150, Noord, tel. 297/8–61666. AE, D, DC, MC, V. No lunch. Closed Sun.*

$$ BRISAS DEL MAR. This friendly, 32-table place overlooking the
★ sea (and accessible from the hotels by bus) makes you feel as if you're dining in an Aruban home. Old family recipes use such indigenous ingredients as the aromatic *yerbiholé* leaf (it has a somewhat minty basil flavor). Try the smashing, steamy fish soup, *keri keri* (shredded fish kissed with annatto seed), or some of the island's best pan bati. The catch of the day cooked Aruban-style (panfried and covered in a tangy creole sauce, or panfried in garlic butter on request) has drawn a crowd for more than 20 years. The terrace is inviting on a breezy night; make reservations early to watch the sunset. (Note that this restaurant participates in the AGA's dine-around program.) *Savaneta 222A, Savaneta, tel. 297/8–47718. AE, MC, V.*

$–$$ EL PATIO. For a quick bite (including breakfast) of cheap local eats, head for this roadside rest stop. Order at the counter and a waitress will bring your food to one of the plastic tables. The creole fish fillets, chicken wings, stoba, tenderloin sandwiches, and other menu items all come with fries, salad, and rice and beans. After your meal, order some *quesillo* (ice cream) and have a game of billiards (the tables are in the back). *Sun Plaza Mall, L. G. Smith Blvd. 160, Oranjestad, tel. 297/8–39192. No credit cards.*

CONTEMPORARY

$$$ L'ESCALE. You're missing out if you don't make a reservation for
★ at least one meal in this upscale eatery (it was rated the island's best in 2000 by the AGA). Sip wine and look out over the bustling L. G. Smith Boulevard while waiting for your sautéed baby snails and Caribbean-style walnut-crusted snapper; for dessert, be

sure to try the rich chocolate soufflé. Sparkles and streamers will decorate your table for a special occasion, and the extensive cigar list can help turn any night into a celebration. If time is short (perhaps you're scurrying off to the Crystal Casino show), opt for the pre-theater menu. *Aruba Sonesta Resort, L. G. Smith Blvd. 82, Oranjestad, tel. 297/8–36000. Reservations essential. AE, D, MC, V. No lunch.*

CONTINENTAL

$$$ CHEZ MATHILDE. This elegant restaurant occupies one of Aruba's last surviving 19th-century houses. Ask to sit in the swooningly romantic Pavilion Room, which has an eclectic mix of Italian and French decor, heavy damask drapes, brass gas lamps, ivy-covered walls, and private nooks and crannies. The back-room greenhouse atrium is an appealing second choice. The outstanding French-style menu is constantly re-created by the Dutch chef, who has a deft touch with sauces. Feast on artfully presented baked escargots, roasted breast of duck on a lentil puree with tamarind sauce and sweet potatoes, ostrich fillet in lightly seasoned breading with sesame and soy dressing on Belgian endive, or quail stuffed with calf's sweetbreads in a bell pepper sauce. The crêpes suzette and chocolate layer cake with mocha and *ponche crema* (Venezuelan eggnog made with brandy) sauce will also please your taste buds. *Havenstraat 23, Oranjestad, tel. 297/8–34968. Reservations essential. AE, DC, MC, V. No lunch Sun.*

$$$ RUINAS DEL MAR. Surrounded by lush landscaping and waterfalls, the "Ruins of the Sea" is the perfect spot for a quiet, romantic dinner—whether you sit in the air-conditioned dining room or on the patio. The exquisite Continental dishes are often given a Caribbean twist. Starters include jerk-spice carpaccio with brandied mayonnaise, peppers, and Parmesan cheese as well as crab cakes with spicy garlic mustard and Caribbean rémoulade. The seafood mixed grill and the grilled veal chop in a shallot and red wine sauce are among the favorite entrées. The Sunday brunch buffet is complete with champagne. Note: a 15% service charge is automatically added to your check. *Hyatt Regency Aruba Beach Resort & Casino, J. E. Irausquin Blvd. 85, Palm Beach, tel. 297/8–61234. AE, D, DC, MC, V. No lunch.*

\$\$–\$\$\$ LE DÔME. ★ Belgian Peter Ballière and his two partners imported 11,000 bricks from Antwerp to authenticate the Continental interior of this fine dining spot. The service is polished, the maroon decor in the main room is sumptuous, and a local harpist and guitarist add considerable ambience. The Belgian endive soup is delicious; the tournedos Rossini (prime-cut beef in a port sauce with a goose-liver mousse), downright decadent. A seven-course set menu is also available. Try one of the eight imported Belgian beers or one of the wine list's 65 varieties. Savor champagne and a cup of coffee with the prix-fixe Sunday brunch. Note that this is a place where shorts are a no-no. *J. E. Irausquin Blvd. 224, Oranjestad, tel. 297/8–71517. Reservations essential. AE, D, DC, MC, V. Closed Mon. and Sept.*

\$\$–\$\$\$ THE PROMENADE. At this upscale spot (it's Aruba's only restaurant with valet parking) you and your significant other can try such appetizers as the crabmeat cocktail, the smoked salmon, or the escargots. Entrées like the filet mignon, T-bone steak, mixed grill, and the fresh catch of the day are prepared to your liking. *Zeppenfeldstraat 15, San Nicolas, tel. 297/8–43131. AE, D, DC, MC, V. Closed Mon.*

CUBAN

\$\$–\$\$\$ CUBA'S COOKIN'. Locals (restaurateurs among them) agree that the food here is "authentic-ethnic." Enter this old *cunucu* (country) house, order a *mojito* (light rum, sugar, mint, and soda) at the bar, and then unwind in the Cuban-art-filled dining room before digging into your truly Cuban dish. *Wilhelminastraat 27, Oranjestad, tel. 297/8–80627. MC, V.*

ECLECTIC

\$\$–\$\$\$ **BAR.COM.** An easy walk from the high-rise hotels, this cybercafé-restaurant serves up cheap, ultrathin pizzas and specialty salads. Order a generic pasta or fish dish for only \$16.95 or skip dinner altogether and play at one of the five iMac computer stations for a nominal fee. *J. E. Irausquin Blvd. 374, Palm Beach, tel. 297/8–63751. AE, D, DC, MC, V. No lunch.*

\$\$–\$\$\$ **CAPTAIN'S TABLE.** If there were an award for the most improved restaurant on Aruba, the Captain's Table—a participant in the AGA's dine-around program—would be a strong contender. After asking the resort's time-share owners for their input, food and beverage director Jerry Mans upgraded the menu—for breakfast, lunch, and dinner—and assembled a top-flight staff. The cuisine is truly eclectic: some Continental, a little Italian, and other types of dishes as well. The nautical-theme decor includes some very attractive fish tanks. *La Cabana All Suite Beach Resort & Casino, J. E. Irausquin Blvd. 250, Eagle Beach, tel. 297/8–79000. AE, MC, V.*

\$\$–\$\$\$ **LAGUNA RESTAURANT.** With its colorful decor, Laguna Restaurant is sure to put you in a vacationing mood. Louvered plantation-style doors frame the view out onto the pond, and you can dine inside (with air-conditioning) or out. A waterside wok, with loads of ingredients to choose from, lets you create your own stir-fry dinner. Breakfast (either buffet or à la carte) is also a possibility. *J. E. Irausquin Blvd. 81, Palm Beach, tel. 297/8–66555. AE, D, DC, MC, V. No lunch.*

\$\$–\$\$\$ **PAPIAMENTO.** Longtime restaurateurs Lenie and Eduardo Ellis
★ converted their 130-year-old home into a bistro that is elegant, intimate, and always romantic. You can feast sumptuously indoors surrounded by antiques or outdoors in a patio garden. The chefs mix Continental and Caribbean cuisines to produce favorites that include seafood and meat dishes. Try the "clay

pot" seafood medley for two. *Washington 61, Noord, tel. 297/8–64544. Reservations essential. AE, MC, V. No lunch. Closed Mon.*

$$–$$$ VENTANAS DEL MAR. The floor-to-ceiling windows of this elegant restaurant look out across a golf course and beyond to rolling sand dunes and the sea off the island's western tip. Dining on the intimate terrace amid flickering candlelight is very romantic. Sandwiches, salads, conch fritters, nachos, and quesadillas fill the midday menu; at night the emphasis is on seafood and meat. The sea bass in orange sauce is a must-try. *Tierra del Sol Golf Course, Malmokweg, tel. 297/8–67800. AE, MC, V.*

$$ QUE PASA. A sign on the wall at the bar welcomes you with a
★ friendly WHAT'S HAPPENING? in different languages. While you wait for your table, select a glass of wine from the list (you'll find it wrapped around one of the bottles set on the bar), check out the local paintings on the walls and decide which one to bring home, and enjoy the aromas from the kitchen. Specialties include lobster bisque, grilled swordfish, ribeye steaks with shiitake mustard sauce, and raspberry pie. The ambience on the dining terrace is sociable; you can hang out here long after dinner and get to know the people at the next table. *Wilhelminastraat 2, Oranjestad, tel. 297/8–33872. AE, D, DC, MC, V. No lunch.*

$–$$ BUCCANEER. Imagine you're in a sunken ship with fishnets hanging above you and sharks, barracudas, and groupers swimming past the portholes. That's the Buccaneer, a virtual underwater grotto—with a fantastic 7,500-gallon saltwater aquarium and 12 porthole-size tanks—snug in an old stone building flanked by heavy black chains. The surf-and-turf dishes are prepared by the chef-owners with European élan. Order the catch of the day, shrimp with Pernod, or smoked pork cutlets with sausage, sauerkraut, and potatoes. Go early (around 5:45 PM) to get a booth next to the aquariums. (Note that this restaurant participates in the AGA's dine-around program.)

Gasparito 11-C, Noord, tel. 297/8–66172. AE, MC, V. No lunch. Closed Sun.

$–$$ COCO PLUM. Grab a newspaper and a *pastechi* (meat-, cheese-, or seafood-filled turnovers) and run, or relax under thatch-roof huts and watch life unfold along Caya Betico Croes. Locals meet here for ham-and-cheese or tuna sandwiches, chicken or steak saté, cheeseburgers, red snapper fillet platters, and chicken wings. Satiate your thirst with an all-natural fruit drink in watermelon, lemon, papaya, tamarind, or passion fruit flavor. At the counter, you can order *loempia* (egg rolls stuffed with vegetables, chicken, or shrimp) or empanas. *Caya Betico Croes 100, Oranjestad, tel. 297/8–31776. No credit cards. No dinner. Closed Sun.*

$–$$ CHARLIE'S RESTAURANT & BAR. Charlie's has been a San Nicolas hangout for more than 50 years. It once drew all kinds of roughs and scruffs, but now tourists flock here to gawk at the decor: the walls and ceiling are *covered* with license plates, hard hats, sombreros, life preservers, baseball pennants, intimate apparel, credit cards—you name it. Decent but somewhat overpriced specialties are Argentine tenderloin and "shrimps jumbo and dumbo" (dumb because they were caught). And don't leave before trying Charlie's special "honeymoon sauce" (so called because it's really hot). The real draw here is the nonstop party atmosphere—an oddly endearing hybrid between that of a frat house and a beach bar. *Zeppenfeldstraat 56, San Nicolas, tel. 297/8–45086. AE, D, MC, V. Closed Sun.*

$–$$ ★ DELIFRANCE. If you're eager to skip the traditional hour-long hotel breakfast, DeliFrance offers the perfect solution. You'll love the freshly baked baguettes, croissants, and other breads. Try the All-American Breakfast Combo (toast with scrambled eggs, bacon, coffee, and fresh OJ) or Le Sweet Bagel (a bagel with cream cheese and jam). Don't leave without tasting the Beukenhorst Koffie, a Costa Rican–blend coffee, and the *poffertjes* (miniature Dutch pancakes often served with melted butter and powdered sugar sprinkled on top). For lunch there's a good selection of salads, sandwiches, and, of course, pastries. Send the kids outside to the play area while you peruse American and European magazines. *Certified Mega Mall, L. G. Smith Blvd. 150, Oranjestad, tel. 297/8–86006. AE, D, MC, V. No dinner.*

$ BREAD BOUTIQUE. Office workers regularly stop by this tiny bread shop for their morning coffee, a bagel, or banana-nut bread. For lunch, enjoy curry chicken sandwiches, crab salad, chicken saté, grilled chicken salad, or fresh fruit salad. Try to get one of the window seats for some people-watching while you eat, or take your food to go. *Sun Plaza Mall, L. .G Smith Blvd. 160, Oranjestad, tel. 297/8–80503. No credit cards. No dinner. Closed weekends.*

FRENCH

$$–$$$ LA BOUILLABAISSE. Named for the celebrated Provençal seafood dish—a specialty here—this restaurant near the high-rise hotels is a good choice when other, better-known places are full. Fishermen's nets full of colorful fish are draped about the place, and there's a small boat right in the middle of the room. Chef Christian Mongellaz, a graduate of the hotel school in Grenoble, France, draws a regular crowd with his Creole-style grouper and his Martha's Vineyard salad (walnuts, sweet onions, soft lettuce, radishes, crumbled blue cheese, and a dressing of maple syrup and raspberry vinegar). For dessert the bananas flambé prepared tableside will mesmerize you. (Note that this restaurant participates in the AGA's dine-around program.) *Bubali 69, Noord, tel. 297/8–71408. AE, MC, V. Closed Tues.*

ITALIAN

$$$ TUSCANY. Oil paintings depicting the Tuscan countryside somehow blend in with the realistic-looking palm trees in this casually elegant restaurant. Two of the chefs have won awards in

Yo, Ho, Ho and a Cake of Rum

When Venancio Felipe Bareno came to Aruba from Spain 50 years ago, little did he know that his family's traditional rum cake recipes would make baking history. His nephew, Franklin Bareno, owner of Bright Bakery, Aruba's largest production bakery, now packages this rum cake for local and international sales. Made with Aruban Palmeira rum, Natural Bridge Aruba's rum cake makes the perfect gift for folks back home. It's available in two sizes, and its history is printed on the side of the box, which is wrapped in vacuum-sealed plastic. It stays fresh for up to six months and is registered in the United States, so you can transport it through customs. At press time, a lower-calorie version was slated to be on the market soon.

the Caribbean Culinary Competition, and their flair and attention to detail are apparent. The *spannochie prima donna con capellini d'angelo* (sautéed shrimp with prosciutto, shallots, wild mushrooms, and artichokes in a light grappa cream on angel hair pasta) is a delight. The excellent service, wine list, and soft piano sounds make for a special evening. *Aruba Marriott Resort and Stellaris Casino, L. G. Smith Blvd. 101, Palm Beach, tel. 297/8–69000. Reservations essential. AE, DC, MC, V. No lunch.*

$$–$$$ PAPARAZZI. The owners of Chez Mathilde (☞ *above*) have put their savvy to work yet again at this gourmet pizza place. The staff is attentive, and the decor is glamorous and romantic: wall sconces and tropical greenery complement the colorful yellow, electric blue, and rich violet color scheme. Choose from fresh, hearty pastas and soups as well as such pies as margherita, Hawaiian, vegetarian, or seafood—all with a thin, crispy crust. There's even an apple pizza (served with a scoop of vanilla ice cream) for dessert. Peer into the glass-enclosed kitchen to see just how the chef gets everything to taste so good. *Seaport Village Marketplace, L. G. Smith Blvd. 9, Oranjestad, tel. 297/8–35966. AE, D, DC, MC, V. No lunch.*

$$–$$$ **RIGOLETTO.** Chef-owner Tino Nicita mastered the art of cooking in his native Taormina, Italy, and diners have enjoyed his authentic Italian dishes for more than 10 years. Generous portions ensure that you walk away satisfied. Start with the antipasto of salami, prosciutto, and cheese or the calamari rings with marinara sauce. Then try the *capellini* (angel hair pasta) sautéed in olive oil with shrimp and bay scallops or the ziti with diced lobster, vodka, tomato sauce, and a touch of heavy cream. Save room for the cannoli. *Bubali 16, Noord, tel. 297/8–37733. AE, MC, V. Closed Mon.*

SEAFOOD

$$–$$$ **FLYING FISHBONE.** This restaurant is a little hard to find, but it's worth the effort for a relaxing beachfront meal. Exotic plants and a Middle Eastern decor transport you back to the days of *Casablanca* as soon as you walk through the door. Reserve a spot on the wooden deck that faces the beach, or dig your toes into the sand at a water's-edge table. Tuna, grouper, and other fresh catches are creatively prepared and artistically presented. The proprietors, who also own Que Pasa (☞ *above*), are definitely doing something right. *Savaneta 344, San Nicolas, tel. 297/8–42506. MC, V. Closed Sun.*

$$–$$$ **WATERFRONT CRABHOUSE.** If you arrived in Aruba on American Airlines, chances are there was a 3,000-plus-pound container of seafood in the belly of your plane. The Waterfront Crabhouse has

The Goods on Gouda

Each year Holland exports more than 250,000 tons of cheese to more than 100 countries, and Gouda (pronounced how-da and named for the city where it's produced) is one of the most popular. Gouda travels well and gets harder, saltier, and more flavorful as it ages. According to Patrick Paris, purchasing director of Consales Aruba, a Gouda wholesaler that sells about 330,000 pounds of cheese each year, there are six types of Gouda: young (at least 4 weeks old), semi-major (8 weeks old), major (4 months old), ultra-major (7 months old), old (10 months old), and vintage (more than 12 months old). When buying cheese, look for the control seal that confirms the name of the cheese, its country of origin, its fat content, and that it was officially inspected.

a contract with York Harbor lobstermen to ship live Maine lobster to Aruba daily, and it has the largest lobster tank in the Caribbean to prove it. Local fishermen also bring their daily catches here. The shrimp baked in a light crust of herbed bread crumbs and Parmesan cheese is served with marmalade and horseradish sauce. The restaurant's superhot lava-rock gas grill sears steak exteriors while leaving their centers juicy. Breakfast or a lunch of burgers or sandwiches is also a possibility. (Note that this restaurant participates in the AGA's dine-around program.) *Seaport Village Marketplace, L. G. Smith Blvd. 9, Oranjestad, tel. 297/8–35858 or 297/8–36767. AE, D, DC, MC, V.*

Weight Conversion Chart

Kilograms/Pounds

To change kilograms (kg) to pounds (lb), multiply kg by 2.20.
To change lb to kg, multiply lb by .455.

kg to lb	lb to kg
1 = 2.2	1 = .45
2 = 4.4	2 = .91
3 = 6.6	3 = 1.4
4 = 8.8	4 = 1.8
5 = 11.0	5 = 2.3
6 = 13.2	6 = 2.7
7 = 15.4	7 = 3.2
8 = 17.6	8 = 3.6

Grams/Ounces

To change grams (g) to ounces (oz), multiply g by .035.
To change oz to g, multiply oz by 28.4.

g to oz	oz to g
1 = .04	1 = 28
2 = .07	2 = 57
3 = .11	3 = 85
4 = .14	4 = 114
5 = .18	5 = 142
6 = .21	6 = 170
7 = .25	7 = 199
8 = .28	8 = 227

STEAK

$$–$$$ **FRENCH STEAKHOUSE.** You can hear the famous "ooh-la-la" chant throughout this well-known restaurant—a participant in the AGA's dine-around program—whenever a delectable steak is set on some lucky diner's plate. People come here from all over the island, and despite reservations, the lines are often out the door at dinnertime. Classical music plays in the background as you dine on hearty steaks, fresh tuna or grouper, and vegetable dishes. The staff couldn't be friendlier. *Manchebo Beach Resort, J. E. Irausquin Blvd. 55, Eagle Beach, tel. 297/8–23444. AE, DC, MC, V. No lunch. Closed Mon.*

It was late in the day when the cruise ship docked. An agitated couple dashed into a jewelry shop and rushed to the gem counter, their shopping clock ticking. "Is anything wrong?" asked the clerk. "Well," said the woman, "our ship was delayed, and now we don't have time to buy all the things we wanted: earrings for my mother, a sarong for my sister, linens for our daughter, and a sculpture for our son." To accommodate the couple—and the other 3,000 passengers—the cruise line extended its stay until midnight and most shops in town remained open.

In this Chapter

shopping

ARUBA'S SOUVENIR AND CRAFTS STORES ARE FULL of Dutch porcelains and figurines, as befits the island's heritage. Dutch cheese is a good buy (you're allowed to bring up to 10 pounds of hard cheese through U.S. customs), as are hand-embroidered linens and any products made from the native aloe vera plant—sunburn cream, face masks, skin refreshers. Local arts and crafts run toward wood carvings and earthenware emblazoned with ARUBA: ONE HAPPY ISLAND and the like.

"Duty free" is a magic term. In fact, about 30% of the island's annual cruise ship visitors teem into the many duty-free stores just steps from the terminal as soon as their ship docks. Most North Americans, who find clothing to be less expensive back home, buy perfume and jewelry; South Americans tend to shell out lots of cash on a variety of brand-name merchandise.

Island merchants are honest and pleasant. Still, if you encounter price markups, unsatisfactory service, or other shopping obstacles, call the tourist office (☞ Practical Information), which will in turn contact the Aruba Merchants Association. A representative of the association will speak with the merchant on your behalf, even if the store isn't an association member.

How and When

It's easy to spend money on Aruba. Most stores accept American currency and Aruban florins (also called guilders; written as Afl) as well as credit cards and traveler's checks. Since there's no sales tax, the price you see on the tag is what you pay. (Note that although large stores in town and at hotels are duty free, in tiny shops and studios, you may have to pay the ABB, or value-added tax, of 6.5%.) Don't try to bargain in stores, where it's considered rude to haggle. At flea markets and vendor stands, however, you might be able to strike a deal.

Shops are open Monday through Saturday 8:30 or 9 to 6. Some stores stay open through the lunch hour (noon–2), and many open when cruise ships are in port on Sunday and holidays. The later you shop in downtown Oranjestad, the easier it will be to park. Also, later hours mean slightly lower temperatures. In fact, the Aruba Merchants Association is trying to get shops to remain open till 8 PM so that visitors who like to spend the day on the beach can come to town and shop in the cool of the evening.

AREAS AND MALLS

Oranjestad's **Caya G. F. Betico Croes** is Aruba's chief shopping street, lined with several duty-free boutiques and jewelry stores noted for the aggressiveness of their vendors on cruise-ship days. Most malls are in Oranjestad and are attractive gabled, pastel-hued re-creations of Dutch colonial architecture.

For late-night shopping, head to the **Alhambra Casino Shopping Arcade** (L. G. Smith Blvd. 47, Manchebo Beach), open 5 PM–midnight. Souvenir shops, boutiques, and fast-food outlets fill the arcade, which is attached to the busy casino. The **Aquarius Mall** (Elleboogstraat 1, Oranjestad) is small but relatively upscale.

If you blink, you might miss the **Dutch Crown Center** (L. G. Smith Blvd. 150 [some shops face Havenstraat], Oranjestad), a small complex with some good finds tucked between the major malls. The **Holland Aruba Mall** (Havenstraat 6, Oranjestad) houses a collection of smart shops and eateries.

Stores at the **Port of Call Marketplace** (L. G. Smith Blvd. 17, Oranjestad) sell fine jewelry, perfumes, duty-free liquor, batiks, crystal, leather goods, and fashionable clothing. The **Royal Plaza Mall** (L. G. Smith Blvd. 94, Oranjestad), across from the cruise-ship terminal, has cafés, a post office (open Monday–Saturday 7–6:45), and such stores as Nautica, Benetton, Tommy Hilfiger, and Gandelman Jewelers. There's also the Internet Café, where you can send e-mail home and get your caffeine fix all in one stop.

Five minutes from the cruise ship terminal, the **Seaport Village Mall** (L. G. Smith Blvd. 82, Oranjestad) includes the Crystal Casino and more than 120 stores, with merchandise to meet every taste and budget. The **Strada I and Strada II** (corner of Klipstraat and Rifstraat, Oranjestad) are shopping complexes in tall Dutch buildings painted in pastels.

SPECIALTY ITEMS
Cigars

You'll find cigars at **La Casa Del Habano** (Royal Plaza Mall, L. G. Smith Blvd. 94, Oranjestad, tel. 297/8–38509). At the **Cigar Emporium** (Seaport Village Mall, L. G. Smith Blvd. 82, Oranjestad, tel. 297/8–25479), the Cubans come straight from the climate-controlled cigar room. Choose from Cohiba, Montecristo, Romeo y Julieta, Partagas, and more. **Superior Tobacco** (L. G. Smith Blvd. 120, Oranjestad, tel. 297/8–23220) is a good place to shop for stogies.

Clothes

Les Accessoires (Seaport Village Mall, L. G. Smith Blvd. 82, Oranjestad, tel. 297/8–36000) sells exclusive leather bags and other items, with prices ranging from $85 to $600. The shop's Venezuelan *pareos* (sarong-like wraps) come in handy as beach cover-ups. Stop by the **Active Boutique** (Dutch Crown Center, Havenstraat 21, Oranjestad, tel. 297/8–37008) for SOS swimsuits made in Brazil. You can pick up a sexy, high-cut two-piece for only $62. Even sexier are the thongs and bikinis in tropical colors. Get creative here by mixing and matching.

Ronchi de Cuba's Aruban Style

"Shopping has recently become tremendously advanced on Aruba," says local fashion designer Ronchi de Cuba. "We're seeing higher-end fashion that's more reasonably priced, from companies like Fendi and Gucci, and the shopping area is still growing." He says the best time to get great buys at the high-end stores is in January, when the holidays are over and the racks are being cleared for the new season.

De Cuba became involved in fashion at age 17, thanks to a high school physical-education assignment where he taught a dance class and presented a show that incorporated theater, choreography, and fashion. After attending college in Miami, Florida, de Cuba returned to his native Aruba to work at a modeling agency. Soon after, he opened his own agency to promote local entertainment and style.

The first Ronchi de Cuba design was a haute-couture number created for Miss Aruba 1999; he has since gone on to create ready-to-wear swimwear, menswear, womenswear, and junior lines. When he's not cutting clothes, the designer travels to New York, Miami, and Paris to peek into the shops and showrooms of major designers.

De Cuba clothes are constructed of fabrics suitable for a warm climate: crepe linens, silk georgettes, and shantungs for day; brocade, wool crepe, crepe de chine, and silk chiffon for evening. Inspired by such designers as John Galliano, Dolce & Gabbana, and Prada, his collections feature playful color schemes that incorporate dark solids, brights, and prints. He turns out a spring-summer collection and a holiday-cruise collection each year and held his first show in the U.S. in 2000. Look for his label at stores in the Seaport Village Marketplace and the Royal Plaza Mall or at his own shop—Revolution—which is under the Club E in Oranjestad.

At **Agatha Boutique** (Seaport Village Mall, L. G. Smith Blvd. 82, Oranjestad, tel. 297/8–37965) splurge on some high-style outfits by New York fashion designer Agatha Brown. At the Agatha Menswear Boutique, you'll find Gregg Norman sportswear, Gianni Versace ties, and Emilio Forli Italian leather belts. **Azucar & Azuquita** (Caya G. F. Betico Croes 49, Oranjestad, tel. 297/8–89849) changes its reasonably priced, high-quality merchandise every three months. Popular items include preshrunk cotton tank tops and T-shirts; men's, women's, and children's sweaters; children's pajamas and bathrobes; and towels. The inventory is organized by color, and everything is neatly folded, wrapped in paper, and placed on whitewashed wooden shelves.

People come to **Caperucita Raja** (Wilhelminastraat 17, Oranjestad, tel. 297/8–36166) for designer baby, children's, and junior clothes as well as a wide selection of shoes. Outfits that cost $21 here sell for about $75 at Saks Fifth Avenue. Forget to pack your intimates? **Colombia Moda** (Wilhelminastraat 19, Oranjestad, tel. 297/8–23460) will help complete your wardrobe with lingerie made of high-quality microfiber fabrics. **Confetti** (Seaport Village Mall, L. G. Smith Blvd. 82, Oranjestad, tel. 297/8–38614) has the hottest European and American swimsuits, cover-ups, hats, and other beach essentials.

Extreme Sports (Royal Plaza Mall, L. G. Smith Blvd. 94, Oranjestad, tel. 297/8–38458) sells everything the sports-aholic could ever need. Invest in a set of Rollerblades or a boogie board or pick up a backpack, bathing suit, or a pair of reef walkers in funky colors. **J. L. Penha & Sons** (Caya G. F. Betico Croes 11/13, Oranjestad, tel. 297/8–24160 or 297/8–24161), a venerated name in Aruban merchandising, sells clothes, perfumes, and cosmetics and offers such brands as Boucheron, Swiss Army, Dior, Cartier, and Givenchy.

At **Mango** (Main St. 9, Oranjestad, tel. 297/8–29700)—part of an international, 500-store franchise—you'll find fashions from as far away as Spain. The embroidered T-shirts at **Rivera Too** (Havenstraat, Oranjestad, tel. 297/8–39249) are classier than those you'll find in many other shops. This is also a good place for accessories.

If the Aruban sun doesn't make your life sizzle, the sexy lingerie at **Secrets of Aruba** (Seaport Village Mall, L. G. Smith Blvd. 82, Oranjestad, tel. 297/8–30897) will. The store also sells oils and lotions that aren't meant for getting a tan. As the many repeat customers will tell you, **Sun + Sand** (Dutch Crown Center, L. G. Smith Blvd. 150, Oranjestad, tel. 297/8–38812) is the place for T-shirts, sweatshirts, polo shirts, and cover-ups.

You'll find innovative active wear at the **Tommy Hilfiger Boutique** (Royal Plaza Mall, L. G. Smith Blvd. 94, Oranjestad, tel. 297/8–38548). Be sure to check out the Tommy Jeans store as well. Menswear reigns supreme at **La Venezolana** (Steenweg 12, Oranjestad, tel. 297/8–21444). You'll find dress separates and suits as well as jeans, shoes, belts, underwear, and socks. Look for such names as Givenchy, Lee Jeans, and Van Heusen.

Wulfsen & Wulfsen (Caya G. F. Betico Croes 52, Oranjestad, tel. 297/8–23823) has been one of the most highly regarded men's and women's clothing stores in Aruba and the Netherlands Antilles for nearly 30 years (and for a century or so in Holland).

Duty-Free Goods

For leather goods (including Bally shoes), perfumes, cosmetics, and men's and women's clothing, stop in at **Aruba Trading Company** (ATC; Caya G. F. Betico Croes 12, Oranjestad, tel. 297/8–22602), which has been in business more than 70 years.

Little Switzerland (Caya G. F. Betico Croes 14, Oranjestad, tel. 297/8–21192; Royal Plaza Mall, L. G. Smith Blvd. 94, Oranjestad, tel. 297/8–34057), the St. Thomas–based giant, has china, crystal, and fine tableware. You'll find good buys on Omega and Rado watches, Swarovski and Baccarat crystal, and Lladro figurines.

At **Weitnauer** (Caya G. F. Betico Croes 29, Oranjestad, tel. 297/8–32503) you'll find specialty Lenox items as well as duty-free fragrances.

Food

The clean, orderly **Kong Hing Supermarket** (L. G. Smith Blvd. 152, Bushiri, tel. 297/8–25545) stocks all the comforts of home—from fresh cuts of meat to prepackaged salads and cole slaw to Lean Cuisine dinners. The liquor section offers everything from exotic liqueurs to beer. There's also a drugstore with name-brand items like Goody hair supplies and Bausch & Lomb eye-care products. The market, which is open Monday–Saturday 8–8 and Sunday 8–1, has an ATM and takes MasterCard and Visa for purchases of $25 or more.

The family-owned and -operated **Ling & Sons Supermarket** (Italiestraat 26, Eagle Beach, tel. 297/8–32370, www.visitaruba.com/ling&sons) is one of the island's top food centers. In addition to a wide variety of grocery items, the supermarket has a Dutch bakery, a deli, a butcher shop, a large produce area, and a well-stocked liquor store. If you plan ahead, the store can have a package of essential foodstuffs delivered to the door of your hotel room in time for your arrival. The market is open 8–8 every day but Sunday.

Gifts and Souvenirs

Art and Tradition Handicrafts (Caya G. F. Betico Croes 30, Oranjestad, tel. 297/8–36534; Royal Plaza Mall, L. G. Smith Blvd. 94, Oranjestad, tel. 297/8–27862) sells intriguing items that look hand-painted but aren't. Buds from the *mopa mopa* tree are boiled to form a resin to which artists add vegetable colors. This resin is then stretched by hand and mouth. Tiny pieces are cut and layered to form intricate designs—truly unusual gifts.

The **Artistic Boutique** (Caya G. F. Betico Croes 25, Oranjestad, tel. 297/8–23142; Wyndham Aruba Beach Resort and Casino,

J. E. Irausquin Blvd. 77, tel. 297/8–64466, ext. 3508; Seaport Village Mall, L. G. Smith Blvd. 82, Oranjestad, tel. 297/8–32567; Holiday Inn Aruba Beach Resort & Casino, J. E. Irausquin Blvd. 230, tel. 297/8–33383) has been in business for 30 years and is known for selling Giuseppe Armani figurines from Italy, usually at a 20% discount; Aruban hand-embroidered linens; gold and silver jewelry; and porcelain and pottery from Spain.

El Bohio (Port of Call Marketplace, L. G. Smith Blvd. 17, Oranjestad, tel. 297/8–29178) will charm you with its wooden-hut display stands holding Arawak-style pottery, Dutch shoes, and wind chimes. You'll also find classic leather handbags. **Creative Hands** (Socotorolaan 5, Oranjestad, tel. 297/8–35665) sells porcelain and ceramic miniature *cunucu* (country) houses and divi-divi trees, but the store's real draw is its exquisite Japanese dolls. Ceramics lovers consider **Kwa Kwa** (Port of Call Marketplace, L. G. Smith Blvd. 17, Oranjestad, tel. 297/8–39471) a souvenir paradise, with wind chimes, pottery, and knickknacks galore—all made of ceramic, of course. Other items include embroidered bags and truly affordable T-shirts.

While you wait (30 minutes) for your film to be developed at **New Face Photo** (Dutch Crown Center, Havenstraat 27, Oranjestad, tel. 297/8–29510) you can shop for gifts. At **Vibes** (Royal Plaza Mall, L. G. Smith Blvd. 93, Oranjestad, tel. 297/8–37949) pick up souvenirs or treat yourself to a Monte Crisco or Cohiba cigar. Clothes from Aruba and Indonesia, hand-painted mobiles, and bamboo wind chimes are among the goodies at **Tropical Wave** (Port of Call Marketplace, L. G. Smith Blvd. 17, Oranjestad, tel. 297/8–21905).

Housewares

Locals swear by **Decor Home Fashions** (Steenweg 14, Oranjestad, tel. 297/8–26620), which sells sheets, bath towels, kitchen towels, place mats, and the like imported from Italy, Germany, Holland, Portugal, and the United States.

Jewelry

In business for 25 years, **Boolchand's** (Seaport Village Mall, L. G. Smith Blvd. 82, Oranjestad, tel. 297/8–30147) fills its 6,000-square-ft space with jewelry, leather goods, watches, sunglasses, games, cameras, and electronics. If green fire is your passion, **Colombian Emeralds** (Seaport Village Mall, L. G. Smith Blvd. 82, Oranjestad, tel. 297/8–36238) has a dazzling array of emeralds, as well as watches by Breitling, Baume & Mercier, Jaeger, Le Coultre, Ebel, Seiko, and Tissot.

Gandelman Jewelers (Royal Plaza Mall, L. G. Smith Blvd. 94, Oranjestad, tel. 297/8–34433) sells Gucci and Rolex watches at reasonable prices, gold bracelets, and a full line of Lladro figurines. **Kenro Jewelers** (Seaport Village Mall, L. G. Smith Blvd. 82, Oranjestad, tel. 297/8–34847 or 297/9–33171) has two stores in the same mall, attesting to the popularity of such merchandise as Mikimoto pearls, the Ramon leopard collection, and various brands of watches.

Leather Goods

Alivio (Steenweg 12-1, Oranjestad, no phone) has shoes for men, women, and children. Whether you're walking around town by day or dressing up for dinner by night you'll find something suitable here. Look for Birkenstock from Germany, Piedro and Wolky from Holland, and Memphisto from France.

If you get lucky, you'll catch one of the year's big sales at **Gucci** (Seaport Village Mall, L. G. Smith Blvd. 82, Oranjestad, tel. 297/8–33952), when prices are slashed on handbags, luggage, wallets, shoes, watches, belts, and ties. Most days, though, don't expect bargains, as prices are comparable to those at the Gucci outlets back home.

Oblivious to the casino's din, a handful of blackjack players are on the edge of their seats. Each has split his or her cards, and there's a lot of money at stake. The dealer's hand totals 16. One player wipes the sweat from his brow; another takes a long drag on her cigarette and slowly exhales. A group of onlookers whisper their predictions. With a flourish, the dealer pulls his final card—a queen! The players shout for joy.

In this Chapter

casinos

THERE WAS A TIME WHEN WOMEN DRESSED in evening gowns and men donned suits for a chic, glamorous night in Aruba's casinos. In the mid-'80s, however, the Alhambra casino opened, touting its philosophy of "barefoot elegance." Suddenly shorts and T-shirts became acceptable attire. The relaxed dress code made gaming seem an "affordable" pastime rather than a luxury.

Today, Aruban casinos attract high rollers, low-stakes types, and non-gamblers alike. Games include slot machines, blackjack (both beloved by North Americans), baccarat (preferred by South Americans), craps, roulette—even sports betting. Theaters, restaurants, bars, and cigar shops have added another dimension to the casinos. Now you can go out for dinner, a show, after-dinner drinks, and gambling all under one roof. In between games, you can get to know other patrons and swap tips and tales.

THE CASINOS

Except for the free-standing Alhambra, most casinos are in hotels; all are on Palm or Eagle Beach or in downtown Oranjestad. Although the minimum age to enter is 18, some venues are relaxed about this rule. By day, barefoot elegance is the norm in all casinos, though many establishments have a shirt-and-shoes requirement and prefer that men avoid wearing tank tops. Evening dress is expected to be more polished, though still casual. In high season, the casinos are open from just before noon to the wee hours; in low season (May to Nov.), they may not start dealing until late afternoon.

If you plan to play large sums of money, check in with the casino upon arrival so that you'll be rewarded for your business. Most hotels offer gambling goodies for patrons, especially large groups of travelers. Complimentary meals at local restaurants, chauffeured tours, and, in the cases of big winners, high-roller suites aren't uncommon provisions. Even small-scale gamblers may be entitled to coupons for meals and discounted rooms.

ALHAMBRA CASINO. Here, amid the Spanish-style arches and leaded glass, a "Moorish slave" named Roger gives every gambler a hearty handshake upon entering. The atmosphere is casual, and with $1 and $2 tables, no one need feel intimidated. Try your luck at blackjack, Caribbean stud poker, roulette, craps, or one of the 300 slot machines that accept American nickels, quarters, and dollars. Head to one of the novelty touch-screen machines, each of which has many games. There's also bingo every Sunday, Monday, Wednesday, and Friday starting at 1 PM. If you fill your card, you can collect the grand prize of a few hundred dollars—not bad for an initial $5 investment. Be sure to sign up for the Alhambra Advantage Card, which gives you a point for each dollar you spend—even if you lose at the tables, you can still go home with prizes. Of course, winners can spend their earnings immediately at the many on-site shops. The casino is owned by the Divi Divi resorts, and shuttle buses run to and from nearby hotels every 15 minutes or so. The slots here open daily at 11 AM; gaming tables operate from noon (in high season) or 6 PM (in low season) till 4 AM. L. G. Smith Blvd. 47, Oranjestad, tel. 297/8–35000, ext. 482.

CASABLANCA CASINO. Smart money is on the Wyndham's quietly elegant casino, which has a Bogart theme and a tropical color scheme. Participate in daily raffles or spend some time at the blackjack, roulette, craps, stud poker, and baccarat tables or the slot machines. Seek out the unique Feature Frenzy machines, which reportedly pay out $6,000 jackpots daily. If gambling isn't your style, venture into the Sirocco Lounge for exotic cocktails, authentic Arabian hookah pipes, and live jazz most nights at 9. Or you can take in the Aruba Carnival Havana Tropical shows. The casino is open daily from noon to 4 AM. *J. E. Irausquin Blvd. 77, Palm Beach, tel. 297/8–64466.*

CENTURION CASINO. Real musical instruments decorate the walls of this small, homey establishment in the Aruba Grand Beach Resort. The clientele is flecked with lawyers and accountants fresh from the States. Like you, they've come to play blackjack, roulette, baccarat, craps, poker, and slots. Look for such theme nights as Lucky Joker Night, when the recipient of a secret joker stashed in a blackjack deck wins a cash prize. The casino opens at 10 AM for slots, 6 PM for all other games; closing time is 2 AM. *J. E. Irausquin Blvd. 79, Palm Beach, tel. 297/8–63900, ext. 149.*

COPACABANA CASINO. The Hyatt Regency's ultramodern Copacabana Casino (open noon–4 AM) is an enormous complex with a Carnival-in-Rio theme that features neon lights, live entertainment, and a marble bar. The most popular games here are slots, blackjack, craps, and baccarat. From 9 PM to 2 AM, toast the Eduardo Maya Band at the stage near the bar, where you'll also find free drinks. Steal away from the pulsating mix of Latin and American tunes and seize your opportunity to become a high roller. Don't forget to register for free dinners and brunches and hotel discounts at the hostess station. *J. E. Irausquin Blvd. 85, Palm Beach, tel. 297/8–61234.*

CRYSTAL CASINO. Open 24 hours a day, 7 days a week, the Sonesta's casino is adorned with Austrian crystal chandeliers and authentic gold-leaf columns that evoke Monaco's grand establishments—hence, the international clientele. The Salon Privé offers serious gamblers baccarat, roulette, and high-stakes blackjack. This is a popular spot for cruise ship passengers, who walk from the port to watch and play in slot

Good Luck Charms

Arubans take myths and superstitions very seriously. They flinch if a black butterfly flits into their home, since this symbolizes death. They gasp if a child crawls under their legs, since it's a sign that the baby won't grow anymore. And on New Year's Eve, they toss the first sips of whiskey, rum, or champagne from the first bottle that's opened in the new year out the door of their house to show respect to those who have died and to wish luck on others. It's no surprise, then, that good luck charms are part of Aruba's casino culture as well.

The island's most common good luck charm is the djucu (pronounced joo-koo), a brown-and-black stone that comes from the sea and becomes hot when you rub it. They're sold at the convenience store near the Natural Bridge (☞ Here and There), and many people have them put in gold settings—with their initials engraved in the metal—and wear them around their necks on a chain with other charms such as an anchor or a cross. Another item that's thought to bring good luck is a small bag of sand. Women wear them tucked discreetly in their bras; one woman who visited Aruba every year always carried a few cloves of garlic in her bag. On a recent visit, she removed the garlic, placed it on a slot machine, and won $1,000 instantly. All the more reason to save the scraps from your salad plate when you leave dinner.

tournaments and bet on sports. The Crystal Lounge, which overlooks the casino, serves up live music as well as cocktails, and the Stardust Theatre's show, *Hot Tickets*, features an international cast of singers and dancers. It also stars Adonis, a white Siberian tiger, who's available for photo ops after the show. *L. G. Smith Blvd. 82, Oranjestad, tel. 297/8–36000.*

EXCELSIOR CASINO. The Holiday Inn Aruba Beach Resort's casino—the birthplace of Caribbean stud poker—has table games, plenty of slot machines, sports betting and a bar with live entertainment (note that drinks are free to anyone at play). It's also the only casino on Palm Beach with an ATM right by the cashier. Games include blackjack, craps, and roulette; there's also a poker room for Texas hold 'em, seven-card stud, and Caribbean stud. Afternoon bingo games overtake the main floor every day. The casino is open daily from 8 AM to 4 AM. *J. E. Irausquin Blvd. 230, Palm Beach, tel. 297/8–67777.*

RADISSON ARUBA CARIBBEAN RESORT. Although its entrance is painted a deep shade of purple and it measures 16,000 square ft, you may have a hard time finding this casino. Descend the stairs at the corner of the resort's lobby, following the sounds of the piano player's tunes. The nightly action here includes Las Vegas–style blackjack, roulette, craps, and slot machines. Overhead, thousands of lights simulate shooting stars that seem destined to carry out your wishes for riches. A host of shops and restaurants afford opportunities for you to chip away at your newfound wealth. The slots here open daily at 10 AM, and the table action begins at 4 PM; everything closes at 4 AM. *J. E. Irausquin Blvd. 81, Palm Beach, tel. 297/8–64045.*

ROYAL CABANA CASINO. The Caribbean's largest casino has a sleek interior, 400 slot machines, no-smoking gaming tables and slot room, and the highest-stakes bingo games around. Its Tropicana Showroom features the *Jewel Box Revue*, in which the "hottest women in Aruba are men." Starring female impersonators who perform as Cher, Madonna, Whitney Houston, Bette Midler, Whoopi Goldberg, and Joan Rivers (to name a few), this Las Vegas–born extravaganza is hosted by Ron Raymond, who changes outfits 17 times in 1½ hours. His rendition of "What Makes a Man a Man" is a showstopper. Performances take place Tuesday, Thursday, and Friday at 9 PM and Wednesday and Saturday at 10 PM. The slots here open at daily at 11 AM, the tables at 5 or 6 PM. The casino closes between 3 AM and 4 AM. *J. E. Irausquin Blvd. 250, Eagle Beach, tel. 297/8–77000.*

ROYAL PALM CASINO. The Allegro Resort's casino opens daily at noon for slots and at 5 PM for all other games. You can hang around till 4 AM, marveling at the colorful 12- by 30-ft mural of famous movie characters as you take your chance at one of 245 slots or at blackjack, roulette, poker, craps, baccarat, and Caribbean stud poker tables. The entire gaming floor joins in the free full-card bingo game held nightly at 10:30. Anyone who scores a full card within the first 50 calls gets a clean grand; everyone who shows a full card after that walks away with a $100 prize. Friday at 8 PM sees a slot tournament, and look for double jackpots daily from 3 PM to 5 PM. *J. E. Irausquin Blvd. 83, Palm Beach, tel. 297/8–69039.*

SEAPORT CASINO. The gambling is low-key at this waterside establishment adjacent to the Aruba Sonesta Suites, the Seaport Marketplace, and the Seaport Conference Center. Slot machines are in daily operation from 10 AM to 4 AM, and tables are open from noon to 4 AM. From here, you can see the boats on the ocean and enjoy not only the games you'd find at other casinos but also shops, restaurants, bars, and movie theaters. The casino's band performs on Friday and Saturday nights from 9 PM to 11 PM. Stop by on Tuesday or Sunday or on the last Saturday night of every month for the casino's popular bingo games. *L. G. Smith Blvd. 9, Oranjestad, tel. 297/8–35027, ext. 4212.*

STELLARIS CASINO. The Marriott's casino has mirrors on the ceilings, and though there's no pink champagne on ice, there are glamorous chandeliers. Start at the slots at noon or the tables at 4 PM and play 'til 4 AM if the action suits you. Take your pick of craps, roulette, Caribbean stud poker, minibaccarat, and Superbuck (like blackjack with suits). The hotel's Tuscany restaurant serves up delectable Italian fare, and Dushi, the Spanish- and American-style casino band, will keep your spirits up no matter how your game is going. Check in with the casino when you arrive at the hotel, and you'll get a membership card and be entered in the computer system. If you play high enough stakes at the tables, you can win free meals and other prizes. If not, you'll at least get a postcard in the mail offering a special rate on future stays. Also note that special hotel rates (a 30% discount) are offered to those who play at least four hours each day of their stay and spend an average of $80 per day on the floor. *L. G. Smith Blvd. 101, Palm Beach, tel. 297/8–69000.*

THE GAMES

For a short-form handbook on the rules, the odds, and the strategies for the most popular casino games—or for help deciding on the kind of action that suits your style—read on.

The first part of any casino strategy is to risk the most money on wagers that present the lowest edge for the house. Blackjack, craps, video poker, and baccarat are the most advantageous to the bettor. The two types of bets at baccarat have a house advantage of a little more than 1%. The basic line bets at craps, if backed up with full odds, can be as low as ½%. Blackjack and video poker can not only put you even with the house (a 50-50 proposition) but give you a slight long-term advantage.

How can a casino provide you with a 50-50 or even a positive expectation at some of its games? First, because a vast number of suckers make bad bets (those with a house advantage of 5%–35%, such as roulette, keno, and slots). Second, because the casino knows that very few people are aware of the opportunities to beat the odds. Third, because it takes skill to exploit these opportunities. However, a mere hour or two spent learning strategies for the beatable games will put you ahead of most visitors who give the gambling industry an average 12%–15% profit margin.

BACCARAT

The most "glamorous" game in the casino, baccarat is a version of *chemin de fer*, which is popular in European gambling halls. It's a favorite with high rollers because thousands of dollars are often staked on one hand. The Italian word *baccara* means "zero." This refers to the point value of 10s and picture cards. The game is run by four pit personnel. Two dealers sit side by side at the middle of the table. They handle the winning and losing bets and keep track of each player's "commission" (explained below). The "caller" stands in the middle of the other side of the table and dictates the action. The ladderman supervises the game and acts as final judge if any disputes arise.

How to Play

Baccarat is played with eight decks of cards dealt from a large "shoe" (or cardholder). Each player is offered a turn at handling the shoe and dealing the cards. Two two-card hands are dealt, the "player" and the "bank" hands. The player who deals the cards is called the banker, although the house banks both hands. The players bet on which hand—player or banker—will come closest to adding up to 9 (a "natural"). Ace through 9 retain face value, while 10s and picture cards are worth zero. If you have a hand adding up to more than 10, the number 10 is subtracted from the total. For example, if one hand contains a 10 and a 4, the hand adds up to 4. If the other holds an ace and a 6, it adds up to 7. If a hand has a 7 and a 9, it adds up to 6.

Depending on the two hands, the caller either declares a winner and loser (if either hand actually adds up to 8 or 9) or calls for another card for the player hand (if it totals 1, 2, 3, 4, 5, or 10). The bank hand then either stands pat or draws a card, determined by a complex series of rules depending on what the player's total is and dictated by the caller. When one or the other hand is declared a winner, the dealers go into action to pay off the winning wagers, collect the losing wagers, and add up the commission (usually 5%) that the house collects on the bank hand. Both bets have a house advantage of slightly more than 1%.

The player-dealer (or banker) holds the shoe as long as the bank hand wins. When the player hand wins, the shoe moves counterclockwise around the table. Players can refuse the shoe and pass it to the next player. Because the caller dictates the action, player responsibilities are minimal. It's not necessary to know the card-drawing rules, even if you're the banker.

Baccarat Strategy

To bet you only have to place your money in the bank, player, or tie box on the layout, which appears directly in front of where you sit. If you're betting that the bank hand will win, you put your chips in the bank box; bets for the player hand go in the player box. (Only real suckers bet on the tie.) Most players bet on the bank hand when they deal, since they "represent" the bank and to do otherwise would seem as if they were betting "against" themselves. This isn't really true, but it seems that way. Playing baccarat is a simple matter of guessing whether the player or banker hand will come closest to 9 and deciding how much to bet on the outcome.

BLACKJACK
How to Play

You play blackjack against a dealer, and whichever of you comes closest to a card total of 21 wins. Number cards are worth their face value, picture cards are worth 10, and aces are worth either 1 or 11. (Hands with aces are known as "soft" hands. Always count the ace first as an 11. If you also have a 10, your total will be 21, not 11.) If the dealer has a 17 and you have a 16, you lose. If you have an 18 against a dealer's 17, you win (even money). If both you and the dealer have a 17, it's a tie (or "push") and no money changes hands. If you go over a total of 21 (or "bust"), you lose, even if the dealer also busts later in the hand. If your first two cards add up to 21 (a "natural"), you're paid 3 to 2. However, if the dealer also has a natural, it's a push. A natural beats a total of 21 achieved with more than two cards.

You're dealt two cards, either face down or face up, depending on the custom of the casino. The dealer also gives herself two cards, one face down and one face up (except in double-exposure blackjack, where both the dealer's cards are visible). Depending on your first two cards and the dealer's up card, you can **stand,** or refuse to take another card. You can **hit,** or take as many cards as you need until you stand or bust. You can **double down,** or double your bet and take one card. You can **split** a like pair; if you're dealt two 8s, for example, you can double your bet and play the 8s as if they're two hands. You can **buy insurance** if the dealer is showing an ace. Here you're wagering half your initial bet that the dealer *does* have a natural. If so, you lose your initial bet but are paid 2 to 1 on the insurance (which means the whole thing is a push). You can **surrender** half your initial bet if you're holding a bad hand (known as a "stiff") such as a 15 or 16 against a high-up card like a 9 or 10.

Blackjack Strategy

Many people devote a great deal of time to learning complicated statistical schemes. However, if you don't have the time, energy, or inclination to get that seriously involved, the following basic strategies should allow you to play the game with a modicum of skill and a paucity of humiliation:

- When your hand is a stiff (a total of 12, 13, 14, 15, or 16) and the dealer shows a 2, 3, 4, 5, or 6, always stand.

- When your hand is a stiff and the dealer shows a 7, 8, 9, 10, or ace, always hit.

- When you hold 17, 18, 19, or 20, always stand.

- When you hold a 10 or 11 and the dealer shows a 2, 3, 4, 5, 6, 7, 8, or 9, always double down.

- When you hold a pair of aces or a pair of 8s, always split.

- Never buy insurance.

CRAPS

Craps is a dice game played at a large rectangular table with rounded corners. Up to 12 players can stand around the table. The layout is mounted at the bottom of a surrounding "rail," which prevents the dice from being thrown off the table and provides an opposite wall against which to bounce the dice. It can require up to four pit personnel to run an action-packed, fast-paced game of craps. Two dealers handle the bets made on either side of the layout. A "stickman" wields the long wooden "stick," curved at one end, which is used to move the dice around the table. The stickman also calls the number that's rolled and books the proposition bets made in the middle of the layout. The "boxman" sits between the two dealers, overseeing the game and settling any disputes.

How to Play

Stand at the table wherever you can find an open space. You can start betting casino chips immediately, but you have to wait your turn to be the shooter. The dice are passed clockwise around the table (the stickman will give you the dice at the appropriate time). It's important, when you're the "shooter," to roll the dice hard enough so they bounce off the end wall of the table. This shows that you're not trying to control the dice with a "soft roll."

Craps Strategy

Playing craps is fairly straightforward; it's the betting that's complicated. The basic concepts are as follows: If the first time the shooter rolls the dice he or she turns up a 7 or 11, that's called a "natural"—an automatic win. If a 2, 3, or 12 comes up on the first throw (called the "come-out roll"), that's termed "craps"—an automatic lose. Each of the numbers 4, 5, 6, 8, 9, or 10 on a first roll is known as a "point": The shooter keeps rolling the dice until the point comes up again. If a 7 turns up before the point does, that's another loser. When either the point or a losing 7 is rolled, this is known as a "decision," which happens on average every 3.3 rolls.

But "winning" and "losing" rolls of the dice are entirely relative in this game, because there are two ways you can bet at craps: "for" the shooter or "against" the shooter. Betting for means that the shooter will "make his point" (win). Betting against means that the shooter will "seven out" (lose). Either way, you're actually betting against the house, which books all wagers. If you're betting "for" on the come-out, you place your chips on the layout's "pass line." If a 7 or 11 is rolled, you win even money. If a 2, 3, or 12 (craps) is rolled, you lose your bet. If you're betting "against" on the come-out, you place your chips in the "don't pass bar." A 7 or 11 loses; a 2, 3, or 12 wins. A shooter can bet for or against himself, herself, or other players.

There are also roughly two dozen wagers you can make on any single specific roll of the dice. Craps strategy books can give you the details on come/don't come, odds, place, buy, big six, field, and proposition bets.

ROULETTE

Roulette is a casino game that utilizes a perfectly balanced wheel with 38 numbers (0, 00, and 1 through 36), a small white ball, a large layout with 11 different betting options, and special "wheel chips." The layout organizes 11 different bets into six "inside bets" (the single numbers, or those closest to the dealer) and five "outside bets" (the grouped bets, or those closest to the players).

The dealer spins the wheel clockwise and the ball counterclockwise. When the ball slows, the dealer announces, "No more bets." The ball drops from the "back track" to the "bottom track," caroming off built-in brass barriers and bouncing in and out of the different cups in the wheel before settling into the cup of the winning number. Then the dealer places a marker on the number and scoops all the losing chips into her corner. Depending on how crowded the game is, the casino can count on roughly 50 spins of the wheel per hour.

How to Play

To buy in, place your cash on the layout near the wheel. Inform the dealer of the denomination of the individual unit you intend to play. Know the table limits (displayed on a sign in the dealer area). Don't ask for a 25¢ denomination if the minimum is $1. The dealer gives you a stack of wheel chips of a different color from those of all the other players and places a chip marker atop one of your wheel chips on the rim of the wheel to identify its denomination. Note that you must cash in your wheel chips at the roulette table before you leave the game. Only the dealer can verify how much they're worth.

Roulette Strategy

INSIDE BETS

With inside bets, you can lay any number of chips (depending on the table limits) on a single number, 1 through 36 or 0 or 00. If the number hits, your payoff is 35 to 1, for a return of $36. You could, conceivably, place a $1 chip on all 38 numbers, but the return of $36 would leave you $2 short, which divides out to 5.26%, the house advantage. If you place a chip on the line between two numbers and one of those numbers hits, you're paid 17 to 1 for a return of $18 (again, $2 short of the true odds).

Betting on three numbers returns 11 to 1, four numbers returns 8 to 1, five numbers pays 6 to 1 (this is the worst bet at roulette, with a 7.89% disadvantage), and six numbers pays 5 to 1.

OUTSIDE BETS

To place an outside bet, lay a chip on one of three "columns" at the lower end of the layout next to numbers 34, 35, and 36. This pays 2 to 1. A bet placed in the first 12, second 12, or third 12 boxes also pays 2 to 1. A bet on red or black, odd or even, and 1 through 18 or 19 through 36 pays off at even money, 1 to 1. If you think you can bet on red *and* black, or odd *and* even, in order to play roulette and drink for free all night, think again. The green 0 or 00, which fall outside these two basic categories, will come up on average once every 19 spins of the wheel.

SLOT MACHINES

Around the turn of 20th century, Charlie Fey built the first slot in his San Francisco basement. Today hundreds of models accept everything from pennies to specially minted $500 tokens. The major advance in the game is the progressive jackpot. Banks of slots within a casino are connected by computer, and the jackpot total is displayed on a digital meter above the machines. Generally, the total increases by 5% of the wager. If you're playing a dollar machine, each time you pull the handle (or press the spin button), a nickel is added to the jackpot.

How to Play

To play, insert your penny, nickel, quarter, silver dollar, or dollar token into the slot at the far right edge of the machine. Pull the handle or press the spin button, and then wait for the reels to spin and stop one by one and for the machine to determine whether you're a winner (occasionally) or a loser (the rest of the time). It's pretty simple, but because there are so many types of machines nowadays, be sure you know exactly how the one you're playing operates.

Slot-Machine Strategy

The house advantage on slots varies from machine to machine, between 3% and 25%. Casinos that advertise a 97% payback are telling you that at least one of their slot machines has a house advantage of 3%. Which one? There's really no way of knowing. Generally, $1 machines pay back at a higher percentage than quarter or nickel machines. On the other hand, machines with smaller jackpots pay back more money more frequently, meaning that you'll be playing with more of your winnings.

One of the all-time great myths about slot machines is that they're "due" for a jackpot. Slots, like roulette, craps, keno, and Big Six, are subject to the Law of Independent Trials, which means the odds are permanently and unalterably fixed. If the odds of lining up three sevens on a 25¢ slot machine have been set by the casino at 1 in 10,000, then those odds remain 1 in 10,000 whether the three 7s have been hit three times in a row or not hit for 90,000 plays. Don't waste a lot of time playing a machine that you suspect is "ready," and don't think if someone hits a jackpot on a particular machine only minutes after you've finished playing on it that it was "yours."

VIDEO POKER

Like blackjack, video poker is a game of strategy and skill, and at select times on select machines, the player actually holds the advantage, however slight, over the house. Unlike with slot machines, you can determine the exact edge of video poker machines. Like slots, however, video poker machines are often tied into a progressive meter; when the jackpot total reaches high enough, you can beat the casino at its own game. The variety of video poker machines is growing steadily. All are played in similar fashion, but the strategies are different. This section deals only with straight-draw video poker.

How to Play

The schedule for the payback on winning hands is posted on the machine, usually above the screen. It lists the returns for a high pair (generally jacks or better), two pair, three of a kind, a flush, full house, straight flush, four of a kind, and royal flush, depending on the number of coins played—usually 1, 2, 3, 4, or 5. Look for machines that pay with a single coin played: 1 coin for "jacks or better" (meaning a pair of jacks, queens, kings, or aces; any other pair is a stiff), 2 coins for two pairs, 3 for three of a kind, 6 for a flush, 9 for a full house, 50 for a straight flush, 100 for four of a kind, and 250 for a royal flush. This is known as a 9/6 machine—one that gives a nine-coin payback for the full house and a six-coin payback for the flush with one coin played. Other machines are known as 8/5 (8 for the full house, 5 for the flush), 7/5, and 6/5.

You want a 9/6 machine because it gives you the best odds: the return from a standard 9/6 straight-draw machine is 99.5%; you give up only half a percent to the house. An 8/5 machine returns 97.3%. On 6/5 machines, the figure drops to 95.1%, slightly less than roulette. Machines with varying paybacks are scattered throughout the casinos. In some you'll see an 8/5 machine right next to a 9/6, and someone will be blithely playing the 8/5 machine!

As with slot machines, it's optimum to play the maximum number of coins to qualify for the jackpot. You insert five coins into the slot and press the "deal" button. Five cards appear on the screen—say, 5, jack, queen, 5, 9. To hold the pair of 5s, you press the hold buttons under the first and fourth cards. The word "hold" appears underneath the two 5s. You then press the "draw" button (often the same button as "deal") and three new cards appear on the screen—say, 10, jack, 5. You have three 5s. With five coins bet, the machine will give you 15 credits. Now you can press the "max bet" button: five units will be removed from your credits, and five new cards will appear on the screen. You repeat the hold and draw process; if you hit a winning hand, the proper payback will be added to your credits. Those who want coins rather than credit can hit the "cash out" button at any time. Some machines don't have credit counters and automatically dispense coins for a winning hand.

Video-Poker Strategy

Like blackjack, video poker has a basic strategy that's been formulated by the computer simulation of hundreds of millions of hands. The most effective way to learn it is with a video poker computer program that deals the cards on your screen, then tutors you in how to play each hand properly. If you don't want to devote that much time to the study of video poker, memorizing these six rules will help you make the right decision for more than half the hands you'll be dealt:

• If you're dealt a completely "stiff" hand (no like cards and no picture cards), draw five new cards.

• If you're dealt a hand with no like cards but with one jack, queen, king, or ace, always hold on to the picture card; if you're dealt two different picture cards, hold both. But if you're dealt three different picture cards, hold only two (the two of the same suit, if that's an option).

• If you're dealt a pair, hold it, no matter the face value.

• Never hold a picture card with a pair of 2s through 10s.

• Never draw two cards to try for a straight or a flush.

• Never draw one card to try for an inside straight.

Clouds fill the sky and a cool breeze blows as the boat
arrives to pick up a group of snorkelers. They board
reluctantly, and their hopes of having an underwater
adventure dim as the skies open in a dramatic downpour.
The boat's bartenders mix up some Captain's Specials
and turn the island music up a notch. This elicits smiles
all around, and the skies seem to brighten. In no time,
the sun is shining again, launching another beautiful day
in the great outdoors.

In this Chapter

outdoor activities and sports

ABOVE THE SEA SURFACE AND BELOW, Aruban waters are brimming with activity. Although beach bumming is a popular pastime, tennis, horseback riding, golf, and fishing are also good options. More adventurous souls can explore on a motorcycle, parasail with the ocean breezes, or leap through the air on a skydive. Constant trade winds have made Aruba an internationally recognized windsurfing destination. The crystalline waters of the island's leeward side offer scuba divers and snorkelers a kaleidoscopic adventure day or night.

You probably won't find Arubans singing "Take Me Out to the Ball Game," but come time for soccer season (late May–November, with matches on Tuesday, Thursday, Saturday, and Sunday) or track-and-field meets and some 3,200 spirited people pack into the **Compleho Deportivo G. P. Trinidad** (Stadionweg, Oranjestad, tel. 297/8–27488). Events at this complex open with the Aruban national anthem, a display of flags, and the introduction of any old-timers in the stadium. Admission ranges from $3 to $6, depending on whether it's a local or international competition. Regardless of what's on, you won't find vendors hawking hot dogs or cotton candy. The snack bar sells such Aruban favorites as *pastechi* (meat, cheese, or seafood-filled turnovers) or *bitterballen* (meatballs) that you can wash down with a soda or a local Balashi beer.

Sidney Ponson: Pitcher

"My life was the beach before baseball," says Sidney Ponson, who started playing ball in Aruba at age nine and signed with the minor leagues at 16 before becoming a right-handed pitcher for the Baltimore Orioles in 1998. Now, he spends 10 months a year in the United States playing and training (his grueling workouts last from 7:30 AM to 1 PM and involve lifting weights, running, and throwing), and two months in Aruba resting and visiting family and friends. The island celebrity, who idolized Roger Clemens throughout his childhood, says he had fun growing up in Aruba, where he loved to sail, scuba dive, and play soccer and volleyball. Baseball was his first passion, though it wasn't easy to play on this dry island, with fields full of rocks. But employment on his uncle's boat taught him to work hard for what he wanted in life.

Trying for the big leagues involved lots of hard work, but it was worth it when he got the call to play. "It was 6:30 AM, and I was on a road trip in a hotel in Scranton," he remembers. "They told me when to show up and said to be ready to play at 8:30." Now there are three other Aruban ballplayers playing in the U.S. (Calvin Maduro, who also plays for the Baltimore Orioles, and Eugene Kingshill and Radames Dijkhoff, who play for Triple A teams), and it won't be long before there are more. To prepare for a game, Ponson heads to the clubhouse for some serious stretching to the hard rock music of Metallica, AC/DC, or Mötley Crüe. How does it feel right before he heads out to pitch? "One million people want to do what I do—play ball in front of 50,000 people every night, and that's a great feeling," he says. Ponson isn't one to set professional goals, preferring to take everything day by day. He does admit that winning a World Series wouldn't be such a bad thing.

BEACHES

The beaches here are legendary: white sand, turquoise waters, and virtually no litter—everyone takes the NO TIRA SUSHI (NO LITTERING) signs very seriously, especially with a $280 fine. The major beaches, which back up to the hotels along the southwestern strip, are public and crowded. Make sure you're well protected from the sun—it scorches fast despite the cooling trade winds. Luckily, there's at least one covered bar (and often an ice cream stand) at virtually every hotel. On the northeastern side, wind makes the waters too choppy for swimming, but the vistas are great, and the terrain is wonderful for exploring.

ARASHI BEACH. The water is calm, the swimming is fine, and the white, powdery sands are shaded by some huts (though there are no other facilities). The beach is a 10-minute walk from the last bus stop on Malmok Beach and is accessible by car or taxi.

BABY BEACH. On the island's eastern tip, this semicircular beach borders a bay that's as placid and just about as shallow as a wading pool—perfect for tots, shore divers, and terrible swimmers. Thatched shaded areas are good for cooling off. Stop by the nearby snack truck for burgers, hot dogs, beer, and soda.

BOCA CATALINA. Although there are some stones and pebbles along this white-sand beach, snorkelers come for the shallow water filled with fish. Swimmers will also appreciate the conditions here. There aren't any facilities nearby, however, so pack provisions.

BOCA GRANDI. Strong swimming skills are a must at this beach near the island's eastern tip.

BOCA PRINS. You'll need a four-wheel-drive vehicle to make the trek here. The beach is about as large as a Brazilian bikini, but with two rocky cliffs and crashing waves, it's as romantic as you get. Boca Prins is also famous for its backdrop of enormous vanilla-sand dunes. This isn't a swimming beach, however. Bring a picnic, a beach blanket, and sturdy sneakers, and descend the rocks that form steps to the water's edge.

BOCA TABLA (BACHELOR'S BEACH). Come to this east-side beach for the white-powder sand and the good snorkeling and windsurfing—not for the swimming (conditions aren't the best) or the facilities (there aren't any).

DOS PLAYA. Hire a four-wheel-drive vehicle, pack a blanket and a picnic basket, and head here to take in the beautiful view. Swimming is discouraged because of strong currents and massive waves.

DRUIF. Fine white sand and calm water makes this "tops-optional" beach a fine choice for sunbathing and swimming. Convenience is a highlight, too: hotels are close at hand, and the beach is accessible by public bus as well as rental car or taxi.

EAGLE BEACH. On the southwestern coast, across the highway from what is quickly becoming known as Time-Share Lane, is what has recently been designated one of the 10 best beaches in the world by *Travel & Leisure* magazine. Not long ago it was a nearly deserted stretch of pristine sand dotted with the occasional thatched picnic hut. Now that the time-share resorts are completed, this mile-plus-long beach hops.

FISHERMAN'S HUT (HADIKURARI). This beach is a windsurfer's haven. In fact, it's the site for the annual Hi-Winds Pro-Am Windsurfing Competition. But any day, you can take a picnic lunch (tables are available) and watch the elegant purple, aqua, and orange sails struggle in the wind. The swimming conditions are good here as well, though the sand has some pebbles and stones.

GRAPEFIELD BEACH. To the northeast of San Nicolas, this sweep of blinding white sand in the shadow of cliffs and boulders is marked by a statue of an anchor dedicated to all seamen. Pick sea grapes in high season (January–June). Swim at your own risk; the waves here can be rough.

MALMOK BEACH. On the northwestern shore, this small, nondescript beach (where some of Aruba's wealthiest families have built tony residences) borders shallow waters that stretch 300 yards from shore. It's the perfect place to learn to windsurf. Right off the coast here is a favorite haunt for divers and snorkelers —the wreck of the German ship *Antilla*, scuttled in 1940.

MANCHEBO BEACH (PUNTA BRABO). In front of the Manchebo Beach Resort (☞ Where to Sleep), this impressively wide stretch of white powder is where officials turn a blind eye to the occasional top-free sunbathers.

MANGEL HALTO (SAVANETA). Drive or cab it over to this east-side beach, a lovely setting for a picnic. Hop into the shallow waters for a swim after taking in the sun on the fine white sand.

PALM BEACH. This stretch runs from the Wyndham Aruba Beach Resort and Casino to the Marriott Aruba Ocean Club (☞ Where to Sleep). It's the center of Aruban tourism, offering the best in swimming, sailing, and other water sports.

RODGER'S BEACH. Next to Baby Beach on the island's eastern tip, this is a beautiful curving stretch of sand only slightly marred by the view of the oil refinery at the bay's far side. Swimming conditions are excellent here, and the snack bar offers live entertainment at the water's edge.

SANTO LARGO. Swimming conditions are good—thanks to shallow water edged by white powder sand—but there are no facilities here.

SURFSIDE. Accessible by public bus, car, or taxi, this beach is the perfect place to swim. It's also conveniently located next to the Havana Beach Club and across the street from the Caribbean Town Beach Resort (☞ Where to Sleep).

ACTIVITIES

ADVENTURE GAMES

Paint-ball aficionados can unite in spirited versions of capture the flag. The game is played with an air gun that propels a biodegradable gelatin capsule, which splatters you with water-soluble paint on impact. To win, simply return the opposing team's flag to your own team's station without being hit by a pellet. Games (complete with equipment and protective gear) are run by **Events in Motion** (Rancho Daimari, Tanki Leendert 249, Plantage Daimari, tel. 297/8–75675 or 297/8–60239). They begin daily at 3 PM, last about two hours, and cost $30 per person with a minimum of 10 people; you must make reservations four days in advance. On-site facilities include a pool, rest rooms, and showers.

BIKING AND MOTORCYCLING

Pedal pushing is a great way to get around the island; the climate is perfect and the trade winds help to keep you cool. **Pablito's Bike Rental** (L. G. Smith Blvd. 234, Oranjestad, tel. 297/8–78655) rents mountain bikes for $15 per day.

If you prefer to exert less energy while reaping the rewards of the outdoors, a scooter is a great way to whiz from place to place. Or let your hair down completely and cruise around on a Harley Davidson. **Big Twin Aruba** (L. G. Smith Blvd. 124-A, Oranjestad, tel. 297/8–28660), which is open Monday through Saturday from 9 to 6, rents Harley Davidson motorcycles to fulfill every biker's fantasy. Rates are $150 for a day, $95 for a half day. The dealership also sells Harley clothing, accessories, and collectibles. Be sure to pose for a photo next to the classic 1939 Liberator on display in the showroom.

For Yamaha scooters, contact **George's Cycle Center** (L. G. Smith Blvd. 124, Oranjestad, tel. 297/9–32202). Other moped, scooter, and motorcycle rental companies are **Donata Car and**

Cycle (Catiri 59, Tanki Leendert, tel. 297/8–34343), **Ron's Motorcycle Rental** (Bakval 17A, Noord, tel. 297/8–62090), and **Semver Cycle Rental** (Noord 22, Noord, tel. 297/8–66851).

BOWLING

The **Eagle Bowling Palace** (Sasakiweg, Pos Abou, Oranjestad, tel. 297/8–35038) has 16 lanes, a cocktail lounge, and a snack bar; it's open daily 10 AM to 2 AM. One lane for one hour will cost you $5.75–$11.50, depending on the time you play; shoes rent for $1.20.

FISHING

Deep-sea catches here include barracuda, kingfish, blue and white marlin, wahoo, bonito, and black and yellow tuna. Each October, the island hosts the International White Marlin Competition. Many charter boats (skippered) are available for half- or full-day sails. Packages include tackle, bait, and refreshments. Prices range from $220 to $320 for a half-day charter, from $400 to $600 for a full day. Contact **De Palm Tours** (L. G. Smith Blvd. 142, Oranjestad, tel. 297/8–24400 or 800/766–6016), **Pelican Watersports** (J. E. Irausquin Blvd. 230, Palm Beach, tel. 297/8–72302), **Red Sail Sports** (J. E. Irausquin Blvd. 83, Oranjestad, tel. 297/8–61603 or 877/733–7245 in the U.S.), or **Teaser Charters** (St. Vincentweg 5, Oranjestad, tel. 297/8–25088).

GOLF

Golf may seem incongruous on an arid island like Aruba, yet there are two courses. The constant trade winds and occasional stray goat add unexpected hazards.

Aruba Golf Club (Golfweg 82, near San Nicolas, tel. 297/8–42006) has a 9-hole course with 20 sand traps and five water traps, roaming goats, and lots of cacti. There are 11 AstroTurf greens, making 18-hole tournaments a possibility. The clubhouse has a bar and locker rooms. The course's official U.S. Golf Association rating is 67; greens fees are $10 for nine holes, $18 for 18 holes. Caddies and club rentals are available.

The **Tierra del Sol** (Malmokweg, tel. 297/8–60978) is on the northwest coast near the California Lighthouse. Designed by Robert Trent Jones Jr., this 18-hole, par-71, 6,811-yard championship course combines Aruba's native beauty—cacti and rock formations—with the lush greens of the world's best courses. The three knockout holes are 3, perched on a cliff overlooking the sea; 14, with a saltwater marsh inhabited by wild egrets; and 16, whose fairway rolls along dunes. The $130 greens fee includes a golf cart; club rentals are $35. Half-day No Embarrassment golf clinics, a bargain at $45, include lunch in the clubhouse. The pro shop is one of the Caribbean's most elegant, with an extremely attentive staff. Package vacations with villa rentals are available.

Two elevated 18-hole miniature golf courses surrounded by a moat are available at **Joe Mendez Miniature Adventure Golf** (Sasakiweg, Noord, tel. 297/8–76625). There are also paddleboats and bumper boats, a bar, and a snack stand. A round of 18 holes costs $6.50, and you can play between 5 PM and 1 AM during the week, from noon on the weekends.

HEALTH CLUB
Corpus Sanus (Certified Mega Mall, L. G. Smith Blvd. 150, Oranjestad) is a cutting-edge fitness club that opened its doors in 2000. With 15,000 square ft of space, this two-floor octagonal-shape gym—created by the fitness gurus at the Gym Source, a New York–based home-gym equipment distributor—has plenty of room for locals and visitors alike. If you come during the day you can take in the beautiful ocean view; if you're a night person note that this place is open 24 hours. The weight-training floor has machines—including fingerprint-access Cybex equipment—and free weights. The second floor has lockers, steam rooms, a sauna, and space for other activities, such as aerobic classes.

HIKING

The Aruban government is working on a 10-year ecotourism plan to preserve the resources of the **Arikok National Park** (tel. 297/8–28001), which makes up 18% of the island's total area and is concentrated in the eastern interior and along the northeast coast. The effort includes setting aside areas for recreation, establishing zones where the natural habitats are protected, and developing a scenic loop roadway. At the park's main entrance, Arikok Center will house offices, rest rooms, and food facilities. Under the new plan, all visitors will have to stop here upon entering so that officials can manage the traffic flow and hand out information on park rules and features.

Hiking in the park, whether alone or in a group led by guides, is generally not too strenuous, although you should exercise caution with the strong sun—bring plenty of water and wear sunscreen and a sun hat or visor. Sturdy, cleated shoes are a must to grip the granular, occasionally steep terrain. There are more than 34 km (20 mi) of trails, and it's important to stick to them. Look for different colors to determine the degree of difficulty. The park is crowned by Aruba's second highest mountain, the 577-ft Mt. Arikok, so climbing is also a possibility.

De Palm Tours (L. G. Smith Blvd. 142, Oranjestad, tel. 297/8–24400 or 800/766–6016) offers a guided three-hour trip to sites of unusual natural beauty that are accessible only on foot. The fee is $25 per person, including refreshments and transportation; a minimum of four people is required.

HORSEBACK RIDING

Four ranches offer short jaunts along the beach or longer trail rides through countryside flanked by cacti, divi-divi trees, and aloe vera plants. Ask if you can stop off at Conchi, a natural pool that's reputed to have restorative powers. Rides are also possible in the

Wildlife Watching

Wildlife abounds on Aruba. Look for the cottontail rabbit: the black patch on its neck likens it to a species found in Venezuela, spawning a theory that it was brought over by pre-Columbian Indians. Wild donkeys, originally transported to the island by the Spanish, are found in the more rugged terrain; sheep and goats roam freely throughout the island.

About 170 bird species make their home on Aruba, and migratory birds (between November and January) temporarily raise the total to 300 species. Among the highlights: the trupiaal (which is bright orange), the prikichi (Aruban parakeet), and the barika geel (a small, yellow-bellied bird with a sweet tooth: you may find one eating the sugar off your table). At Bubali Bird Sanctuary on the island's western side, you can see various types of waterfowl, especially cormorants, herons, scarlet ibis, and fish eagles. Along the south shore, brown pelicans are common. At Tierra del Sol golf course in the north, you may glimpse the shoko (endangered burrowing owl).

Lizard varieties include large iguanas, once hunted (a practice that's now illegal) for use in local soups and stews. Like chameleons, iguanas change color to adapt to their surroundings—from bright green when in foliage (which they love to eat) to a brownish shade when on the soil. The pega pega lizard—a cousin of the gecko—is named for the suction pads on its feet that allow it to grip virtually any surface ("pega" means "to stick" in Papiamento). The kododo blauw (whiptail lizard) is unique to the island.

There are two types of snakes found only on Aruba. The cat-eyed santanero is a harmless variety that won't, however, hesitate to defecate in your hand should you pick it up. The poisonous cascabel is a unique subspecies of rattlesnake that doesn't use its rattle. These snakes live in the area between Mt. Yamanota, Fontein, and San Nicolas.

Arikok National Wildlife Park. Rates run from $25 for an hour-long trip to $65 for a 3½-hour tour. Private rides cost slightly more.

De Palm Tours (L. G. Smith Blvd. 142, Oranjestad, tel. 297/8–24400 or 800/766–6016) can arrange treks. Ranches include **Rancho del Campo** (Sombre 22E, tel. 297/8–50290), **Rancho Daimari** (Plantage Daimari, tel. 297/8–60239), **Rancho Notorious** (Boroncana, Noord, tel. 297/8–60508), and **Rancho el Paso** (Washington 44, tel. 297/8–73310).

JET SKIING

Sputter around Aruba's aqua-blue waters on jet skis. Rentals are available at most hotel water-sports centers. Average prices are $45 for 30 minutes' use of a single jet ski and $55 for 30 minutes' use of a double. Or try **De Palm Tours** (L. G. Smith Blvd. 142, Oranjestad, tel. 297/8–24400 or 800/766–6016), **Pelican Watersports** (J. E. Irausquin Blvd. 230, Palm Beach, tel. 297/8–72302), **Red Sail Sports** (J. E. Irausquin Blvd. 83, Oranjestad, tel. 297/8–61603 or 877/733–7245 in the U.S.), or **Unique Sports of Aruba** (L. G. Smith Blvd. 79, Oranjestad, tel./fax 297/8–60096 or 297/8–63900).

KAYAKING

Kayaking is a popular sport on Aruba's calm waters. **De Palm Tours** (L. G. Smith Blvd. 142, Oranjestad, tel. 297/8–24400 or 800/766–6016) offers the Aruba Kayak Adventure—a four-hour guided kayaking tour with lunch and snorkeling Monday–Saturday; the cost is $65.

PARASAILING

Motorboats from Palm and Eagle beaches tow people up and over the water for about 12 minutes ($45 for a single-seater, $75 for a tandem). There's no official center where you can make arrangements, just independent operators stationed on the beaches. **Caribbean Parasail** (tel. 297/8–60505) is one operator you can call.

SAILING

You can have a hull of a good time Sunfish sailing in Aruba, or you can opt for a day or sunset sail aboard a trimaran or catamaran. The **Seaport Marina** (Seaport Marketplace 204, Oranjestad, tel. 297/8–39190) offers charters.

Other cruise operators include **De Palm Tours** (L. G. Smith Blvd. 142, Oranjestad, tel. 297/8–24400 or 800/766–6016), *Mi Dushi* (Turibana Plaza, Noord 124, Noord, tel. 297/8–28919), **Pelican Watersports** (J. E. Irausquin Blvd. 230, Palm Beach, tel. 297/8–72302), **Red Sail Sports** (J. E. Irausquin Blvd. 83, Oranjestad, tel. 297/8–61603 or 877/733–7245 in the U.S.), *Tattoo* (Turibana Plaza, Noord 124, Noord, tel. 297/8–23515), *Wave Dancer* (Ponton 88, Noord, tel. 297/8–25520), and *Windfeathers* (Rooi Santo 5D, Noord, tel. 297/8–28919).

SCUBA DIVING AND SNORKELING

With visibility of up to 90 ft, Aruban waters are excellent for snorkeling and diving. Both advanced and novice divers will find their niche here, as many of the sites are in shallow waters ranging in depths of 30 ft to 60 ft. Shipwrecks and reefs are inhabited by a colorful and diverse menagerie of sea life, including several varieties of coral, fish—from grunts to groupers—sensuously waving sea fans, giant sponge tubes, gliding manta rays, sea turtles, lobsters, octopuses, and green moray eels. Note that marine preservation is a priority on Aruba, and in 1995, the adoption of CITES (Conference on International Trade in Endangered Species) regulations made it unlawful to remove coral, conch, and other marine life from the water.

Most resorts offer courses for beginners (including equipment); divers seeking advanced certification can do so through any of the island's internationally licensed dive centers. Some dive sites are listed below, but be sure to pick up the Aruba Tourism Authority's brochure, "The Island for Water Sports," which describes many more.

Operators

Expect snorkel gear to rent for about $15 per day and trips to cost around $40. Scuba rates are around $40 for a one-tank reef or wreck dive, $65 for a two-tank dive, and $45 for a night dive. Resort courses (introduction to scuba diving) average $70; complete open-water certification costs around $300.

Dive operators include **Aruba Pro Dive** (Ponton 88, Noord, tel. 297/8–25520), **Dax Divers** (Kibaima 7, Santa Cruz, tel. 297/8–51270), **De Palm Tours** (L. G. Smith Blvd. 142, Oranjestad, tel. 297/8–24400 or 800/766–6016), **Dive Aruba** (Williamstraat 8, Oranjestad, tel. 297/8–25216), **Mermaid Sport Divers** (Manchebo Beach Resort, J. E. Irausquin Blvd. 55A, Eagle Beach, tel. 297/8–35546), **Native Divers Aruba** (Koyari 1, Noord, tel. 297/8–64763), **Pelican Watersports** (J. E. Irausquin Blvd. 230, Palm Beach, tel. 297/8–72302), **Red Sail Sports** (J. E. Irausquin Blvd. 83, Oranjestad, tel. 297/8–61603 or 877/733–7245 in the U.S.), **Scuba Aruba** (Seaport Village Mall, L. G. Smith Blvd. 82, Oranjestad, tel. 297/8–34142), **SEAruba Fly and Dive** (Shiribana 9A, Paradera, tel. 297/8–78759), and **Unique Sports of Aruba** (L. G. Smith Blvd. 79, Oranjestad, tel. 297/8–60096 or 297/8–63900).

Sites on the West Side

ANTILLA **WRECK.** This German freighter off the northwest coast near Malmok Beach is popular with divers and snorkelers. Scuttled during World War II when it was brand-new, the 400-ft-long *Antilla*—referred to by locals as "the ghost ship"—has large compartments. You can also climb into the captain's bathtub, which is beside the wreck, for a unique photo op. Lobster, angelfish, yellow tail, and other fish swim about the wreck, which is blanketed by giant tube sponges and coral.

BARCADERA REEF. Only large types of coral—staghorn, elkhorn, pillar—find their niche close to this reef island because the sand makes it difficult for the smaller varieties to survive. The huge (and abundant) sea fans here are also memorable.

BLACK BEACH. The clear waters here are dotted with sea fans, lobster, and fish. The area takes its name from the rounded black stones lining the shore. It's the only bay on the island's north coast sheltered from thunderous waves, making it a safe spot for diving.

***CALIFORNIAN* WRECK.** The steamer that received—but failed to respond to—SOS signals from the sinking *Titanic* was later stranded on Aruba's rocky northwest coast. Although the ship is submerged at a depth that's perfect for underwater photography, this site is good only for advanced divers; the currents here are strong, and the waters are dangerously choppy.

HARBOUR REEF. Steeply sloped boulders surrounded by a multitude of soft coral formations in calm waters make this a great spot for novices. It's also noteworthy for its abundance of fascinating plant life.

MALMOK REEF. Lobsters and stingrays are among the highlights at this bottom reef adorned by giant green, orange, and purple barrel sponges as well as leaf and brain coral. From here, you can see the *Debbie II*, a 120-ft barge sunk in 1992.

***PEDERNALES* WRECK.** During World War II, this oil tanker was torpedoed by a German submarine. The U.S. military cut out the damaged centerpiece, towed the two remaining pieces to the States, and welded them together into a smaller vessel that eventually transported troops during the Normandy invasion. The section that was left behind is now surrounded by coral formations in shallow water, making this a good site for novice divers. The ship's cabins, wash basins, and pipelines are exposed, and the area teems with grouper and angelfish.

Paris, France.

Paris, Texas.

When it Comes to Getting Local Currency at an ATM, Same Thing.

Whether you're in Yosemite or Yemen, using your Visa® card or ATM card with the PLUS symbol is the easiest and most convenient way to get local currency. For example, let's say you're in France. When you make a withdrawal, using your secured PIN, it's dispensed in francs, but is debited from your account in U.S. dollars. This makes it easy to take advantage of favorable exchange rates. And if you need help finding one of Visa's 627,000 ATMs in 127 countries worldwide, visit **visa.com/pd/atm**. We'll make finding an ATM as easy as finding the Eiffel Tower, the Pyramids or even the Grand Canyon.

It's Everywhere You Want To Be®.

SEE THE WORLD
IN FULL COLOR

Fodors Exploring Guides bring all the great sights vividly to life with hundreds of photographs, fascinating historical background, and colorful anecdotes. Detailed maps and practical information keep you headed in the right direction.

Pair a Fodor's Exploring Guide with your trusted Fodor's Pocket Guide for a complete planning package.

Fodors EXPLORING GUIDES

At bookstores everywhere.

SKELETON CAVE. Human bones found here (historians hypothesize that they're ancient Arawak Indian remains) gave this dive spot its name. A large piece of broken rock forms the entrance where the cave meets the coast.

SONESTA REEF. Near Sonesta Island are two downed planes that make an interesting dive site. Several types of brain coral abound in this sandy bottom area.

TUGBOAT WRECK. At the foot of the Harbour Reef, gradually dropping to about 80 ft, this highly photogenic dive site is one of Aruba's most popular. Spectacular formations of brain, sheet, and star coral blanket the path to the wreck, which is inhabited by a pair of bright green morays.

Sites on the East Side

CAPTAIN ROGER **WRECK.** A plethora of colorful fish swish about this old tugboat, which rests off the coast at Seroe Colorado. From shore you can access a steep coral reef nearby.

ISLA DI ORO. Here, a wide expanse of reef grows far out along the shallow bank, making for superb diving. You'll be treated to views of green moray eels; coral crabs; French, gray, and queen angelfish; trumpet fish; and snapper.

JANE **WRECK.** This 200-ft freighter is in an almost vertical position at a depth of 90 ft just outside the coral reef west of Palm Island. Night diving is very colorful here, as the polyps emerge from the corals that grow profusely on the steel plates of the decks and cabins. Soft corals and sea fans are also abundant here.

PALM ISLAND. Accessible only by boat and secluded behind clusters of mangrove, this reef system stretches far and wide, all the way to Oranjestad. The variegated marine life here makes it a colorful dive site, and you can get close enough to touch the nurse sharks that sleep tucked into reef crevices during the day.

PUNTA BASORA. This narrow reef stretches far into the sea off the island's easternmost point. On calm days, you'll see eagle rays, stingrays, barracuda, hammerhead sharks, tuna, ballyhoo, and dorado as well as hawksbill and loggerhead turtles.

SHARK CAVES. Here you can swim alongside sand sharks and the sleeping nurse sharks.

VERA **WRECK.** In 1954, this freighter sank while en route from South America to North America. The crewmen, who were saved by an Aruban captain, claimed that the cargo consisted of Nazi valuables.

THE WALL. During their egg-laying season (May–August), green sea turtles abound at this steep wall reef. The seascape includes long-branched gorgons, groupers, and burrfish. Close to shore, massive sheet corals are plentiful; in the upper part of the reef, coral varieties include black, star, and flower. Throughout, brain, grooved, knobby, ribbon, and scroll coral grow, and jackknife fish are right at home beneath the mounds. Flitting about are brilliant damselfish, rock beauties, and porgies.

SKYDIVING

You can fall head over heels for Aruba as you tandem jump from 10,000 ft. Jumps are offered early in the morning seven days a week by **Skydive Aruba** (Paradera 211, Paradera, tel. 297/8–35067 or 297/9–37151). To make the leap, you must be over 18 years old, under 240 pounds, and in good health. This remarkable two-hour experience costs $220.

TENNIS

Aruba's winds make tennis a challenge even if you have the best of swings. Although nonguests can make arrangements to play at the resorts, court priority goes to guests. Some private tennis clubs also welcome visitors. Try the world-class facilities at the **Aruba Racquet Club** (Rooisanto 21, Palm Beach, tel. 297/8–60215). Host to a variety of international tournaments, the club

Yani Brokke: Olympic Athlete

The Olympics wouldn't have been the same without Yani Brokke, a 71-year-old Aruban who started playing soccer at age 7 and has since represented the island in Olympic basketball, tennis, baseball, and soccer. Says the multitalented athlete, "I like sports, and they like me, too. I can try a sport for the first time and in two days I can play." He has played in packed stadiums, received merits and ribbons from the government, and has been decorated with medals by Queen Beatrix herself. "In the old days, there wasn't much to do on Aruba," says Brokke. "Life was all about school and sports. Today, kids are involved in computers, TV, sports, and parties as well as other distractions." Despite his success, the often self-coached Brokke believes he was born too early. "There was a lot of good talent but a lack of guidance, and aspiring athletes needed people to back them up. These days, good players get coaches and have a little more direction." After all these years, Brokke is still in the game: he gives tennis lessons at the Bushiri Hotel every weekday afternoon.

has eight courts (six lighted), as well as a swimming pool, an aerobics center, and a restaurant. Fees are $10 per hour; a lesson with a pro costs $20 for a half hour, $35 for one hour.

WINDSURFING

Whisk through the waves and revel in the sea spray. Aruba has all it takes for windsurfing: trade winds that average 15 knots year-round (they peak May–July); a dry, sunny climate; and picture-perfect azure blue waters. With a few lessons from a certified instructor, even novices will be jibing in no time. The southwestern coast's tranquil waters make it ideal for both beginners and intermediates, as the winds are steady but sudden gusts rare. Experts will find the Atlantic coast, especially

Some Wind, Some Lose

Want to rip with (or just watch) the best windsurfers? Every June sees the Aruba Hi-Winds competition, with professional and amateur participants from around the world. There are divisions for women, juniors, men, masters, and grand masters. Disciplines include slalom, course racing, long distance, and free-style. The entry fee is $150 (there's a $25 discount if you register on-line at www.aruba-hiwinds.com), which includes a jersey, lunches, dinners, and parties. As a registrant, you're also entitled to discounts from sponsors, which include car rental companies and hotels. Throughout the weeklong event, there are lots of festivities for both athletes and spectators.

around Grapefield and Boca Grandi beaches, more challenging; winds are fierce and often shift course without warning. Rentals average about $60 a day, and lessons range from $45 to $75. Many hotels include windsurfing in their water sports packages, and most operators can help you arrange complete windsurfing vacations.

The **Aruba Windsurfing Academy** (L. G. Smith Blvd. 462, Malmok Beach, tel. 297/8–62527 or 800/252–1070 in the U.S. to arrange packages through Sailboard Vacations) offers first-rate instruction. It's at Windsurf Village, a lodging complex created by and for windsurfers near Fisherman's Huts, a world-renowned sailing spot. Another lure for those in the know: the complex is home to one of the Caribbean's largest and best-stocked windsurfing shops.

Other operators include **Fisherman's Huts Windsurf Center** (Aruba Marriott Resort, L. G. Smith Blvd. 101, Palm Beach, tel. 297/8–69000), **Pelican Watersports** (J. E. Irausquin Blvd. 230, Palm Beach, tel. 297/8–72302), **Roger's Windsurf Place** (L. G. Smith Blvd. 472, Malmok Beach, tel. 297/8–61918), **Sailboard Vacations** (L. G. Smith Blvd. 462, Malmok Beach, tel. 297/8–61072), **Vela Aruba** (Palm Beach, tel. 297/8–69000 ext. 6430).

Hooiberg loomed before the adventure-seeker. Water bottle in hand, he gingerly began his ascent. His breath grew shorter as he made his way up. Within 15 minutes he reached the top and paused to take in a view that stretched all the way to Venezuela. Leonardo DeCaprio's line in Titanic flashed through his mind: "I'm the king of the world!" On the way down, he encountered a group about to embark on the same journey. "Piece of cake," he offered, nodding toward the hill. Then he headed back to his hotel for a massage.

In this Chapter

here and there

ARUBA'S WILDLY SCULPTED NATURAL BEAUTY is replete with rocky deserts, cactus jungles, secluded coves, blue vistas, and the trademark divi-divi tree. To preserve the environment while encouraging visitors to explore, the government has implemented the first phases of a 10-year, $10 million ecotourism plan. Initiatives include finding ways to make efficient use of the limited land resources and protecting the natural and cultural resources in such preserves as Arikok National Park and the Coastal Protection Zone (along the scenic north and east coasts).

Oranjestad, Aruba's capital, is good for shopping by day and dining by night, but the "real Aruba"—with its wild, untamed beauty—can be found only in the countryside. Rent a car, take a sightseeing tour, or hire a cab for $30 an hour (for up to four people). Though desolate, the windward (northern and eastern) shore is striking and well worth a visit. A drive out past the California Lighthouse (in the northwest) or to Seroe Colorado (in the southeast) will give you a feel for the backcountry.

Although the main highways are well paved, the windward side still has some roads that are a mixture of compacted dirt and stones. A car is fine, but a four-wheel-drive vehicle will enable you to navigate the unpaved interior. Note that few beaches outside the hotel strip along Palm and Eagle beaches to the west have refreshment stands, so pack your own food and drink. Also, aside from those in the infrequent restaurant, there are no public bathrooms outside of Oranjestad.

Traffic is sparse, but signs leading to sights are often small and hand-lettered (this is slowly changing as the government puts up official road signs), so watch closely. Route 1A travels southbound along the western coast, and 1B is simply northbound along the same road. If you lose your way, just follow the divi-divi trees.

Numbers in the margin correspond to points of interest on the Exploring map.

WESTERN ARUBA

Western Aruba is where you'll spend most of your time. All the resorts and time-shares are here, most of them clustered on the oceanfront strip at the luscious Palm and Eagle beaches, in the city of Oranjestad, or in the district of Noord. All the casinos, major shopping malls, and most restaurants are in this region as well, as is the airport.

A Good Tour

Rent a car and head out on Route 1A toward **Oranjestad** ① for a couple hours of sightseeing and shopping. Then drive inland along Route 6A, passing the town of Paradera. Pick up Route 4A and follow it a short way to the **Ayo and Casibari Rock Formations** ②. Continue on 4A and follow the signs for **Hooiberg** ③ (Haystack Hill); if you're so inclined, climb the steps for an outrageous view. Return to 6A and drive a couple of miles to the Bushiribana Gold Smelter. Beyond it on the windward coast is the **Natural Bridge** ④. You'll have to veer off 6A (which bends east here); follow the signs.

Retrace your drive to Route 6; take 6B to the intersection of Route 3B, which you'll follow into the town of **Noord** ⑤, a good place to stop for lunch. Then take Route 2B (briefly), and follow the signs for the branch road to the **Alto Vista Chapel** ⑥. Return to town and pick up 2B and then 1B to reach the **California Lighthouse** ⑦. In this area you'll also see Arashi Beach (a popular snorkeling site) and the Tierra Del Sol golf course. From the lighthouse follow 1A back toward Palm Beach. On the way, stop at the **Butterfly Farm** ⑧, **De Olde Molen** ⑨, and the **Bubali Bird Sanctuary** ⑩.

TIMING

If you head out right after breakfast, you can just about complete the tour above in one very full day. If you want to linger in Oranjestad's shops or in the museums or you want to stop for long swims or a snorkel session, consider breaking the tour up into two days.

What to See

❻ ALTO VISTA CHAPEL. Alone near the island's northwest corner sits the scenic little Alto Vista Chapel. The wind whistles through the simple mustard-color walls, eerie boulders, and looming cacti. Along the side of the road back to civilization are miniature crosses with depictions of the stations of the cross and hand-lettered signs exhorting PRAY FOR US, SINNERS and the like—a simple yet powerful evocation of faith. To get here, follow the rough, winding dirt road that loops around the island's northern tip or, from the hotel strip, take Palm Beach Road through three intersections and watch for the asphalt road to the left just past the Alto Vista Rum Shop.

❷ AYO AND CASIBARI ROCK FORMATIONS. The massive boulders at Ayo and Casibari are said to be a mystery, since they don't match the island's geological makeup. You can climb to the top for fine views of the arid countryside, cacti, and passing Aruba whip-tail lizards—the males are cobalt blue, the females blue with dots. The main path to Casibari has steps and handrails (except on one side), and you must move through tunnels and on narrow steps and ledges to reach the top. At Ayo you'll find ancient pictographs in a small cave (the entrance has iron bars to protect the artifacts from vandalism). You may also encounter a local boulder climber, one of many who are increasingly drawn to

Map labels:

- California Pt.
- Arashi Beach
- Californian Wreck
- **7**
- Boca Catalina
- Malmok Reef
- Malmok Beach
- Antilla Shipwreck
- Debbie II
- Fisherman's Hut (Hadi Kurrari)
- **8**
- Pedernales Wreck
- **9**
- Palm Beach
- **5**
- **10**
- Eagle Beach
- Manchebo Beach (Punta Brabo)
- Druif Beach
- Harbour Reef
- L. G. Smith Blvd
- Oranjestad
- Druif Bay
- Tugboat Reef
- Sonesta Reef
- Barcadera Reef
- Surfside Beach
- Mt. Altovista
- **6**
- Bushiribana
- Bushiribana Gold Smelter
- Tanki Leendert
- Paradera **2**
- **3**
- Santa Cruz
- Aeropuerto Internacional Reina Beatrix
- 1 A/B
- 1 A/B
- 2 A/B
- 3 A/B
- 4 A/B
- 6 A/B
- 7 A/B
- Skeleton Cave
- Jane Wreck
- The Wall
- Palm Reef
- **1**
- N
- 0   4 miles
- 0   6 km

KEY

⊁ beaches
🛳 cruise ship terminal
◣ dive sites
❶ sights

Black Beach
Andicouri
Arikok National Park
Mt. Arikok
Dos Playa
Boca Prins
Fontein Cave
Miralamar
Guadirikiri Cave
Bananca Sunu
Masiduri Cave
Mt. Yamanota
Balashi Gold Mill Ruins
Spanish Lagoon
Boca Grandi
Balashi Brewery
Boca Table (Bachelor's Beach)
Reef
Mangel Halto (Savaneta)
Natural Bridge
Captain Roger Wreck
Mangel Halto Reef (Pos Chiquito Reef)
Santo Largo Beach
Grapefield Beach
Shark Caves
Isla di Oro
Rodger's Beach
Vera Wreck
Punta Basora
Baby Beach

7 A/B
7B
7A
4 A/B
4 A/B
7B
1 A/B
1A

Ayo's smooth surfaces. Access to Casibari is via Tanki Highway 4A to Ayo via Route 6A; watch carefully for the turnoff signs near the center of the island on the way to the windward side.

⓾ BUBALI BIRD SANCTUARY. Bird-watchers delight in the more than 80 species of migratory birds that nest in this wetlands area inland from the high-rise hotels. Herons, egrets, cormorants, coots, gulls, skimmers, terns, and ducks are among the winged wonders in and around the two interconnected man-made lakes that compose the sanctuary. J. E. Irausqin Blvd., Noord, no phone. Free. Daily.

❽ BUTTERFLY FARM. Hundreds of butterflies from around the world flutter about this spectacular garden. Guided 20- to 30-minute tours (included in the price of admission) provide an entertaining look into how these creatures complete their life cycle: from egg to caterpillar to chrysalis to butterfly. There's a special deal offered here: after your initial visit, you can return as often as you like for free. J. E. Irausquin Blvd., Palm Beach, tel. 297/8–63656. $10. Daily 9–4:30 (last tour at 4).

❼ CALIFORNIA LIGHTHOUSE. The lighthouse, built by a French architect in 1910, stands at the island's far northern end. Although its interior is closed to the public, you can ascend the hill to its base for some great views. It's surrounded by huge boulders that look like extraterrestrial monsters and sand dunes embroidered with scrub that resemble tawny, undulating sea serpents. In this stark landscape you'll feel as though you've just landed on the moon. Next to the nearby Trattoria El Farro Blanco—a great place to watch the sun set—there's a placard explaining the lighthouse's history and the wreck of a German ship (just offshore here).

❸ HOOIBERG. Named for its shape (*hooiberg* means "haystack" in Dutch), this 541-ft peak lies inland just past the airport. Climb the 562 steps to the top for an impressive view of Oranjestad. On a clear day, you can even see the coast of Venezuela.

❹ NATURAL BRIDGE. Centuries of raging wind and sea sculpted this coral rock bridge in the center of the windward coast. To reach it, follow the main road inland (Hospitalstraat) and then follow the signs. Just before you reach the natural bridge, you'll pass the massive, intriguing stone ruins of the Bushiribana Gold Smelter, which resembles a crumbling fortress, and a section of surf-pounded coastline called Boca Mahos. Near the natural bridge are a souvenir shop and a café overlooking the water.

❺ NOORD. The district of Noord is home to a strip of high-rise hotels and casinos along Palm Beach; the beautiful St. Ann's Church, with its handmade altar; and the Tierra del Sol golf course. In this area Aruban-style homes are scattered amid cacti.

❾ DE OLDE MOLEN. This windmill's history dates from 1804, when the original was built in Friesland, Holland, to pump water from land below sea level. Damaged by a storm in 1878, it was taken apart and then reconstructed in another location in Holland, where it was used to mill grains. Half a century later, it was damaged once again by a storm and remained idle from 1929 until 1960, when a Dutch merchant purchased its wooden frame. It was shipped piece by piece to Aruba and rebuilt atop a two-story concrete structure in 1974. It now houses a museum—containing Dutch antiques, local farming implements, and a traditional horse-and-carriage display—and the Mill Restaurant (closed Sunday), which serves fresh local seafood, beef, chicken, veal, and a special Dutch pea soup at moderate prices. A bar at the museum is open until 4 AM, so you can dance and party at this unique setting all night long. *L. G. Smith Blvd. 330, Noord, tel. 297/8–66300 or 297/8–62060. Free.*

❶ ORANJESTAD. Aruba's charming capital is best explored on foot. Its central, palm-lined thoroughfare runs between old and new pastel-painted buildings of typical Dutch design (Spanish influence is also evident in some of the architecture). There are many malls with boutiques and shops; downtown and Seaport

Divi-Divi Tree

Like a statuesque dancer in a graceful flat-back pose, the watapana, or divi-divi tree, is one of Aruba's hallmarks. This tropical shrub, the Caesalpinia coriaria, is a member of the legume family. Its astringent pods contain high levels of tannin, which is leached out for tanning leather. The pods also yield a black dye. The tree has a moderate rate of growth and a high drought tolerance. Typically it reaches no more than 25 ft in height, with a flattened crown and irregular, forked branches. Its leaves are dull green, and its inconspicuous yet fragrant flowers are pale yellow or white and grow in small clusters. Thanks to constant trade winds the divi-divis serve as a natural compass: they're bent toward the island's leeward, or western, side, where most of the hotels are.

Village are the major shopping areas. Every morning, the wharf teems with activity as merchants sell produce and fresh fish—often right off their boats. You can also buy handicrafts and T-shirts at this dockside bazaar, where bargaining is expected and dollars or florins are accepted. Island schooners and houseboats anchored near the fishing boats add to the port's ambience. Wilhelmina Park, a small tropical garden on the waterfront along L. G. Smith Boulevard, has a sculpture of the Netherlands' Queen Wilhelmina, whose reign lasted from 1890 to 1948.

At the **Archaeological Museum of Aruba** you'll find two rooms chock-full of fascinating Indian artifacts, farm and domestic utensils, and skeletons. *J. E. Irausquinplein 2A, tel. 297/8–28979. Free. Weekdays 8–noon and 1–4.*

One of the island's oldest edifices, **Ft. Zoutman** was built in 1796 and played an important role in skirmishes between British and Curaçao troops in 1803. The Willem III Tower, named for the Dutch monarch of that time, was added in 1868 to serve as a lighthouse. Over time, the fort has also been put to use as a government office building, a police station, and a prison. Now its historical museum displays Aruban artifacts in an 18th-century house. *Zoutmanstraat, tel. 297/8–26099. Free. Weekdays 8–noon and 1–4.*

The tiny **Numismatic Museum,** next to the St. Francis Roman Catholic Church, displays coins and currencies—some of it salvaged from shipwrecks in the region. The museum was spawned by one Aruban's private collection and is now family run. Some of the coins on display circulated during the Roman Empire, the Byzantine Empire, and the ancient Chinese dynasties; a few date as far back as the 5th century BC. *Zuidstraat 7, tel. 297/8–28831. Free. Weekdays 7:30–noon and 1–4:30.*

Built in 1962, **Beth Israel Synagogue** is the only synagogue on Aruba, and it strives to meet the needs of its Ashkenazi, Sephardic, European, North American, and South American worshipers. The island's Jewish community dates back to the opening of the oil refinery in the 1920s, and at first, congregations met in private homes in San Nicolas. The temple holds regular services on Friday at 8 PM—followed by a kiddush—and on Saturday at 8 AM; additional services are held on holidays and by request. Visitors are always welcome, though it's best to make an appointment to see the synagogue outside of services. A Judaica shop sells keepsakes; at press time, there were plans to add kosher dry goods and kiddush wines to the stock. *Adrian Laclé Blvd. 2, tel. 297/8–23272. Free except high holy days, when tickets ($50) are required.*

EASTERN ARUBA

In addition to the vast Arikok National Park, eastern Aruba is home to the island's second largest city, San Nicolas, and several charming fishing villages and pristine beaches. Here you'll get a real sense of island life.

A Good Tour

Take Route 1A to Route 4B and visit the Balashi Gold Mill Ruins and **Frenchman's Pass** ⑪. Return to 1A and continue your drive past Mangel Halto Beach to **Savaneta** ⑫, a fishing village and one of several residential areas with examples of typical Aruban homes. Follow 1A to **San Nicolas** ⑬, where you can meander along the main promenade, pick up a few souvenirs, and grab a bite to eat. Heading out of town, continue on 1A until you hit a fork in the road; follow the signs toward **Seroe Colorado** ⑭, with the nearby natural bridge and the Colorado Point Lighthouse. From here, follow the signs toward Rodgers Beach, just one of several area beaches where you can kick back for a while. Nearby Baby Beach, with calm waters and beautiful white sand, is a favorite spot for snorkelers. To the north, on Route 7B, is Boca Grandi, a great windsurfing spot. Next is Grapefield Beach, a stretch of glistening white sand against a backdrop of cliffs and boulder formations. Shortly beyond it on 7B, you'll come into **Arikok National Park** ⑮, where you can explore caves and tunnels, play on sand dunes, and stop at Mt. Yamanota, Aruba's highest elevation. Farther along 7B is Santa Cruz, where a wooden cross stands atop a hill to mark the spot where Christianity was introduced to the islanders. The same highway will bring you all the way into Oranjestad.

TIMING

You can follow the tour and see many of the sights in a half day, though it's easy to fill a full day if you spend time relaxing on a beach or exploring Arikok National Park.

What to See

⑮ ARIKOK NATIONAL PARK. Nearly 20% of Aruba has been designated part of this national park, the keystone of the government's long-term ecotourism plan. Most of it sprawls across the interior, stretching to the north and encompassing a long strip of windward shore. Near the island's center and within the confines of the park is Mt. Arikok, the heart of a natural preserve that showcases the island's flora and fauna, the ruins of a gold-mining operation at Miralmar, and the remnants of Dutch peasant settlements at Masiduri. The 620-ft Mt. Yamanota, Aruba's highest peak, is also in the park.

Anyone looking for geological exotica should head for the park's **caves** on the northeastern coast. Baranca Sunu, the so-called Tunnel of Love, has a heart-shape entrance and, within, naturally sculpted rocks that look like the Madonna, Abe Lincoln, and even a jaguar. The Guadirikiri and Fontein caves are marked with ancient drawings (rangers are on hand to offer explanations), as both were used by native Indians centuries ago. Bats are known to make appearances (but don't worry—they won't bother you). Although you don't need a flashlight (paths here are well lighted), it's best to wear sneakers.

⑪ FRENCHMAN'S PASS. Overhanging trees and towering cacti border this luscious stretch of road. The pass is almost midway between Oranjestad and San Nicolas; follow L. G. Smith Boulevard past a shimmering vista of blue-green sea, and turn off where you see the drive-in theater (a popular local hangout). Then drive to the first intersection, turn right, and follow the curve to the right. Gold was discovered on Aruba in 1824, and near Frenchman's Pass are the massive cement-and-limestone ruins of the **Balashi Gold Smelter** (take the dirt road that veers to the right), a lovely place to picnic and listen to the parakeets. A magnificent, gnarled divi-divi tree guards the entrance. The area now is home to Aruba's desalination plant, where all of the island's drinking water is produced.

⑬ SAN NICOLAS. During the heyday of the oil refineries, Aruba's oldest village was a bustling port; now it's dedicated to tourism. The main promenade is full of interesting kiosks, and the whole district is undergoing a revitalization project that will introduce parks, a cultural center, a central market, a public swimming pool, and an arts promenade. The institution in town is **Charlie's Restaurant & Bar** (☞ Eating Out), a hangout for more than 50 years. Stop in for a drink and advice on what to see and do.

⑫ SAVANETA. The Dutch settled here after retaking the island in 1816, and it was Aruba's first capital. Today, it's a bustling fishing village with a 150-year-old *cas de torto* (mud hut), the oldest house still standing on the island.

⑭ SEROE COLORADO. What was originally built as a community for oil workers is an eerie oasis of calm, with an intriguing 1939 chapel. The site is surreal: organ pipe cacti—nearly as tall as the refinery's belching smokestacks—form the backdrop for sedate whitewashed cottages. The real reason to come here is the second, "secret" **natural bridge.** Keep bearing east past the community, continuing uphill until you run out of road. You can then hike down to the cathedral-like formation. It's not too strenuous, but watch your footing, and be sure to follow the white arrows painted on the rocks—there are no other directional signs. Although this bridge isn't as spectacular as its celebrated sister, the raw elemental power of the sea that created it, replete with hissing blow holes, certainly is.

Cunucu Houses

Pastel houses surrounded by cacti fences adorn Aruba's flat, rugged cunucu ("countryside" in Papiamento). The features of these traditional houses were developed in response to the environment. Early settlers discovered that slanting roofs allowed the heat to rise and small windows helped to keep in the cool air. Among the earliest building materials was caliche, a durable calcium carbonate substance found in the island's southeastern hills. Many houses were also built using interlocking coral rocks that didn't require mortar (this technique is no longer used, thanks to cement and concrete). Contemporary design combines some of the basic principles of the earlier homes with touches of modernization: windows, though narrow, have been elongated; roofs are made of bright tiles; patios have been added; and doorways and balconies present an ornamental face to the world beyond.

There's a traffic jam on L. G. Smith Boulevard—it's 11 PM on Friday and everyone is trying to make his or her way into Oranjestad. A cab pulls into the Havana Club parking lot, weaving through swarms of scantily clad women and casually dressed men. The pulse of Oreo, the island's most famous band, and an air of anticipation grip the nightcrawlers waiting to get in. Only when the oversize door swings open does the night really begin.

In this Chapter

nightlife

ALTHOUGH THE RESORT BARS HERE OFTEN turn up the volume when the sun sets, unlike on many other islands, Aruban nightlife isn't confined to touristy hotel folkloric shows. In addition to spending time in one of the many casinos (☞ Casinos), you can slowly savor a drink while the sun dips into the sea, dance to the beat of a local band, bar-hop by bus, or simply stroll along a deserted starlit beach.

How and When

Arubans like to party (the more the merrier), and they usually start celebrating late. The action (mostly on weekends) doesn't pick up 'til around midnight. Casual yet trendy attire is the norm. Most bars don't have a cover charge, though the nightclubs do. Bigger clubs, such as Club E and Havana Club, have lines on weekends, but they move quickly; use this time to start your socializing and you may just end up with a dance partner before you even step foot inside the door. Drink specials are available at some bars, and the Balashi Cocktail (the local term for a glass of water) is always free. Both bars and clubs have either live bands or DJ music depending on the night.

No matter where you choose to party, be smart about getting back to your hotel. Drinking and driving is against the law. Taxis are a good option. If you're in walking distance, go ahead and hoof it. The island is safe, and you'll probably wander with swarms of other visitors in town and along Palm Beach.

Sources

For information on specific events check out the free magazines *Aruba Nights*, *Aruba Events*, *Aruba Experience*, and *Aruba Holiday*, all available at the airport and at hotels.

BAR-HOPPING BUSES

A uniquely Aruban institution is the **Kukoo Kunuku** (tel. 297/8–62010), a psychedelically painted '57 Chevy bus. Weeknights, as many as 40 passengers board to carouse six local bars from sundown to midnight, with a refueling stop for dinner. Group and private charter rates are available; these include picking you up (and pouring you off) at your hotel. Reservations are essential, and the $55 per-person fee covers pick-up (6 PM), drop-off, dinner, and drinks.

While trekking around town, you may spot a colorful, hand-painted, open-air 1947 Ford F500 bus called the **Bonbini Chiva Paranda** (tel. 297/8–25353). Hop aboard and visit Aruba's favorite hangouts. You'll be escorted from bar to bar to get a taste of authentic Aruban nightlife. Trips take place Tuesday and Thursday from 6:30 PM to 12:30 AM; call for reservations. Rates are $45 per person.

BARS

Catch a glimpse of the elaborate swimming pool with whirlpools, waterslides, and waterfalls from the **Alfresco Lobby Bar** (Hyatt Regency Aruba Beach Resort & Casino, J. E. Irausquin Blvd. 85, Palm Beach, tel. 297/8–61234, ext. 4265) while sipping premium wine or a tropical cocktail. This is where Hyatt guests gather nightly to hear live music and stop by for a nightcap after leaving the casino. Many visitors, including those on party-bus tours, find their way to **Carlos & Charlie's** (Weststraat 3A, Oranjestad, tel. 297/8–20355), which may be why locals shy away from it. You'll find mixed drinks by the yard; Mexican fare; American music from the '60s, '70s, and '80s; and a mike-toting

A Bartender's Life

Albert Tromp, celebrity bartender, has been mixing drinks and pulling pints on Aruba for 30 years. He started as a barback at the Aruba Caribbean, then worked for the Manchebo Beach Hotel, the Sheraton, and the Americana, where he was head bartender for six years. Tromp also ran his own restaurant for 2½ years. He received a degree from the Bushiri Hotel School and eventually returned to the bartending life he preferred. He's now the beverage manager at the Radisson—where the glassware is oversize, the cocktails are creative, and the wine list is extensive.

"In the '70s, I sold tons of martinis," says Tromp. Now, drinks with exotic names and flavors seem to be in favor. Folks come from everywhere, for example, to sample his famous Albert Special (also known as the Key Banana Blast), a combination of local liquors like Poncha Crema (coconut cream), rum, crème de banana, and blue Curaçao poured in the bottom and down the sides. If you overindulge, ask Tromp to prepare you one of his secret hangover curatives.

Tromp has organized cocktail competitions and was instrumental in establishing the Aruba Bar Association. He also helped to define the taste of Aruba's Balashi beer—the island's first local brew—by sitting on the panel that conducted tastings for color, foam, and flavor. "Tourists would always come to the bar and ask to try the local beer, and we would serve Amstel, which is brewed on Curaçao, since that was the closest thing we had," says Tromp. His bartending highlights have included glimpses of Chuck Norris and Kenny G. as well as a visit from Sinbad (he drank VO and water, and his crew put down lots of Jack Daniels), who was filming a movie in Venezuela and came to the island for the weekend with about 2,000 people.

emcee. Set in a former fisherman's house behind Royal Plaza Mall, **Castaway's** (Schelpstraat 43, Oranjestad, tel. 297/8–33649) is a popular restaurant-bar. The beer is cold, the service is cheerful, and the all-you-can-eat ribs are famous around the island.

In business since 1948, **Cheta's Bar** (Paradera 119, Paradera, tel. 287/8–23689), formerly known as Flor di Oriente Bar, is a real local joint that holds no more than four customers at a time. There aren't any bar stools, either, which is why most patrons gather in front. During the Saturday-afternoon happy hour, people mingle in the street and lean on their cars while sipping Balashi beer ($1.35) and munching on Bright Bakery buns. No one even seems to mind that, without a permit, Cheto's can't serve mixed drinks and it must close by 9 PM (it opens at 8:30 AM, though).

Drive into Seroe Colorado, on the far side of Rodger's Beach, and you'll see a two-level deck overlooking the crystal-clear blue bay. **Coco Beach Bar & Restaurant** (Rodger's Beach, Seroe Colorado, tel. 297/8–43434) is a popular spot for food and drinks day or evening.

Galley Bar & Lounge (La Cabana All Suite Beach Resort & Casino, J. E. Irausquin Blvd. 250, Eagle Beach, tel. 297/8–79000) serves late-afternoon and evening cocktails and occasionally features live music. **Iguana Joe's** (Royal Plaza Mall, L. G. Smith Blvd. 94, Oranjestad, tel. 297/8–39373) has a creative reptilian-theme decor and a color scheme featuring such planter's-punch colors as lime and grape.

Jimmy's Place (Kruisweg 15, Oranjestad, tel. 297/8–22550) is a smoky Dutch bar that attracts all types—from bankers and lawyers to the staff from other bars. Happy hour on Friday is a good time to stop by, sip a cocktail, smoke a stogie, and unwind. The after-hours crowd often turns up here for soups and sandwiches. The laid-back beachfront **Kokoa** (Palm Beach, tel. 297/8–62050) is often full of beauties in skimpy bathing suits

Balashi Brewery

There was a time when you could walk into any Aruban bar, ask for a Balashi cocktail (referring to the area where the island's water plant is located), and get a glass of water. But since the creation of the local Balashi beer, such a drink order now has a whole new meaning. Made by a German brewmaster in a state-of-the-art brewery using prime hops and malt, Balashi has an alcohol content of 5% and is like a Pilsner lager. Everyone on the island is asking for it. "It's a big tourist thing," explains Gerben Tilma, general manager of the plant. "Everyone wants to know what the best local products are. Now we can tell them."

The **Balashi Brewery** (Balashi, tel. 297/8–54805) has free 30-minute tours (every half hour between 10 am and 2 pm daily), a souvenir shop, a restaurant-café, and a 10,000-square-ft beer garden where you can enjoy a cold one.

and windsurfer guys in shorts. It's a popular Sunday evening spot, and Tuesday is reggae night.

Mambo Jambos (Royal Plaza Mall, 2nd fl., L. G. Smith Blvd. 94, Oranjestad, tel. 297/8–33632) is daubed in sunset colors, with parrots painted on the ceiling. It offers several house-specialty libations, and you can buy Mambo Jambos memorabilia at a shop next door. With front-row seats to view the green flash—that ray of light that flicks through the sky as the sun sinks into the ocean—the **Palms Bar** (Hyatt Regency Aruba Beach Resort & Casino, J. E. Irausquin Blvd. 85, Palm Beach, tel. 297/8–61234) is the perfect sunset spot.

The atmosphere at **Salt & Pepper** (J. E. Irausquin Blvd. 370A, Palm Beach, tel. 297/8–63280) is a mixture of Dutch and Latin

American. Come for the wide variety of tapas and the good selection of reasonably priced Chilean wines. Set atop Boonoonoonoo's restaurant (☞ Eating Out), **Tzapagaga** (Wilhelminastraat 18A, Oranjestad, tel. 297/8–31888) attracts locals and visitors (there's always a crowd) with its eclectic drinks and tasty finger food.

CRUISES

On the *Jolly Rodger* **Sunset Cruise** (tel. 297/8–62010) you can walk the plank, witness a pirate wedding, sing a pirate tune, or just have some snacks and polish off another Jolly Rodger Wicked Rum Punch at the open-air bar—all as the sun sets. The catamaran departs from the Aruba Grand Beach Resort pier Monday, Wednesday, and Friday at 5 PM for a two-hour trip. The cost is $25 per person; call for reservations.

Don't be surprised if you're enjoying a romantic ocean-view dinner on Palm Beach and you see a twinkle of lights on the horizon. It may be the *Tattoo* (tel. 297/8–62010) party boat, a catamaran that sails every night but Sunday from 8 to midnight. It has three decks for dancing (there are live bands and a DJ), dining, and star-gazing. End the evening with the famous Tattoo rope swing. The $49 per-person fee includes dinner; reservations are required.

DANCE AND MUSIC CLUBS

The **Bushiri Beach Resort Pool Bar** (L. G. Smith Blvd. 35, Punta Brabo, tel. 297/8–25216) isn't just for lounging. On Friday night, the Popcorn dancers perform at 9 PM, and the music continues 'til 11 PM. Any other night, stop by for live music between 7 and 11. At **Café Bahia** (Weststraat 7, Oranjestad, tel. 297/8–89982) an elegant spiral staircase leads up to a bar and dance floor backed by a mural of colorful cacti against a blue, cloud-smattered Aruban sky. Locals and tourists drink cocktails and salsa to music provided by island bands.

Live bands perform at the **Cellar** (Klipstraat 2, Oranjestad, tel. 297/8–28567) Monday and Thursday–Saturday; the music du jour might be blues, jazz, funk, reggae, or rock.

The exotic **Club E** (Bayside Mall, Westraat 5, Oranjestad, tel. 297/8–87474) has a huge stainless-steel dance floor that doesn't fill up till after 1 AM, walls decorated with hair-dryer tubes and slinkies, bartenders in hard hats, and a cozy VIP lounge. The crowd—which is always eager to hear the local band Crystal Breeze—is as eclectic as the club's managing director, Anthony Muyale. There's a $5 cover charge.

The energy is high 'til closing time at **Club 2000** (Royal Plaza Mall, 2nd fl., L. G. Smith Blvd. 82, Oranjestad, tel. 297/8–89450), owing to a crowd made up of mostly young guys and girls who live for American rap. The music blasts, the lights pulsate, and the dance floor and circular bar throb to the movement of the crowds. The cover charge is $5.

La Fiesta (Aventura Mall, Plaza Daniel Leo, Oranjestad, tel. 297/8–35896), an upscale indoor-outdoor space, attracts a casual yet classy crowd. A couple of laps around the wraparound terrace overlooking the square at the head of the main street gives night owls a chance to scope the black-clad crowd. Inside, heavy red curtains add drama, and although there's no dance floor, owner David Nataf insists on playing a cool mix of rock that inspires patrons to bop at the bar as they sip. The cover charge is $5. Stop by the cozy **Sirocco Lounge** (Wyndham Aruba Beach Resort and Casino, L. G. Smith Blvd. 77, Palm Beach, tel. 297/8–64466) for jazz performances every evening except Wednesday and Sunday.

For jazz and local music, try the **Garufa Cocktail Lounge** (Wilhelminastraat 63, Oranjestad, tel. 297/8–27205), a cozy cigar bar that also serves as a lounge for customers awaiting a table at El Gaucho Argentine Grill (☞ Eating Out) across the street (you're issued a beeper so that the restaurant can notify

Cool Concoctions

These drink recipes come from Aruban-born bartender Clive Van Der Linde.

● **THE WOW.** Mix equal parts (2 ounces or so) of rum and vodka as well as triple sec, a splash of tequila, grenadine, coconut cream, and pineapple and orange juice. Quips Van Der Linde, "You won't taste the alcohol, but after two, you'll feel pretty good."

● **THE IGUANA.** Mix equal parts of rum, vodka, and add either blue Curaçao or blue grenadine for color. Add crème de banana liqueur, coconut cream, and pineapple juice. Says Van Der Linde, "I learned this one more than 10 years ago on the first sailing boat I worked on. It was called the Balia, which means 'to dance.' "

● **THE CAPTAIN'S SPECIAL.** Mix equal parts of rum and vodka, and add a splash of amaretto, crème de banana, and pineapple and orange juice. "It's really simple," says Van Der Linde. "Just blend with crushed ice, and it's ready to drink."

you when your table is ready). While you wait, have a drink from the extensive list, enjoy some appetizers, and take in the striking decor (leopard-print carpet, Nicole Miller–style bar stools). The smooth ambience may draw you back for an after-dinner cognac.

The Equators and Champagne 2000, two local bands, are always in the spotlight at the beach-side **Gilligan's** (Radisson Aruba Caribbean Resort, J. E. Irausquin Blvd. 81, Palm Beach, tel. 297/8–66555) bar. You'll feel like you've been shipwrecked on an island as you sip tropical drinks here.

The funky **Havana Club** (L. G. Smith Blvd. 1, Oranjestad, tel. 297/8–80557) could have been designed by the creator of the *Friends* set. The purple walls are adorned with gold-frame mirrors, antique lanterns, and dried flowers. The two oversize dance floors are often packed on weekends; Wednesday's Ladies Night (women get in free, men pay the usual cover charge of $15) draws a crowd of about 3,000. The music alternates between pop, rock, and international hits; local bands, including longtime favorite Oreo, sometimes play here. Take refuge from the crowds on a patio complete with a bar, a small swimming pool, and a private stretch of beach.

On Wednesday and Friday–Sunday, you can catch Supermania, one of Aruba's most celebrated bands, at **Pata Pata** (La Cabana All Suite Beach Resort & Casino, J. E. Irausquin Blvd. 250, Eagle Beach, tel. 297/8–79000). The band Steel & Strings plays during extended happy hours on Tuesday and Thursday. Live music nightly makes the **Pelican Terrace** (Divi Aruba Beach Resort, J. E. Irausquin Blvd. 45 , tel. 297/8–23300) a popular nightspot. Sip creative cocktails, dance around the pool, and grab a late-night snack—perhaps a pizza hot from the wood-burning oven.

Two local bands alternate their stints at **Rick's Café American** (Wyndham Aruba Beach Resort and Casino, J. E. Irausquin Blvd. 77, Palm Beach, tel. 297/8–64466), where fruity cocktails and refreshing beers are always available. As the bar is in the Wyndam's casino, you can throw a quarter in the slots on your way in—you just might win enough to cover your bar tab. At the **Stellaris Lounge & Lobby Bar** (Aruba Marriott Resort and Stellaris Casino, L. G. Smith Blvd. 101, Palm Beach, tel. 297/8–69000) nightly entertainment is provided by a local band that gets the party started at about 9 PM and keeps it going till at least 2 AM.

MOVIES

The **Seaport Cinema** (Seaport Market Place, tel. 297/8–30318) has six theaters showing the latest American movies in English. The earliest shows are around 4 PM; late shows start around 10:30 PM. Ticket prices range from $5.50 to $7.

Temperature & Liquid Volume Conversion Chart

Temperature: Metric Conversions

*To change Centigrade or Celsius (C) to Fahrenheit (F),
multiply C by 1.8 and add 32. To change F to C, subtract 32
from F and multiply by .555.*

C°	F°	F°	C°
0	-17.8	60	15.5
10	-12.2	70	21.1
20	-6.7	80	26.6
30	-1.1	90	32.2
32	0	98.6	37.0
40	+4.4	100	37.7
50	10.0		

Liquid Volume: Liters/U.S. Gallons

*To change liters (L) to U.S. gallons (gal), multiply L by .264.
To change U.S. gal to L, multiply gal by 3.79.*

L to gal	gal to L
1 = .26	1 = 3.8
2 = .53	2 = 7.6
3 = .79	3 = 11.4
4 = 1.1	4 = 15.2
5 = 1.3	5 = 19.0
6 = 1.6	6 = 22.7
7 = 1.8	7 = 26.5
8 = 2.1	8 = 30.3

Check out the not-so-silver screen under the stars at the **E. de Veer Drive-In Theater** (Kibaima, tel. 297/8–58355). It will cost you about $3 (buy your tickets at the entrance) to watch the English-language movies from your parked car—speakers alongside—on this massive screen set in a field near Balashi off Route 1A/1B. Movies start at 8:30 PM. The drive-in can accommodate about 100 cars and has a snack bar.

THEME NIGHTS

At last count there were more than 30 theme nights offered during the course of a week. Each "party" features a buffet dinner, entertainment (usually of the limbo, steel-band, stilt-walking variety), and dancing. The top groups tend to rotate among the resorts. For a complete list contact the Aruba Tourism Authority (☞ Practical Information). Best bets are the **Aruba Extravaganza** (Manchebo Beach Resort, J. E. Irausquin Blvd. 55, Eagle Beach, tel. 297/8–23444) on Friday, the **Havana Tropical** (Wyndham Aruba Beach Resort and Casino, J. E. Irausquin Blvd. 77, Palm Beach, tel. 297/8–64466) on Saturday, and **Caribbean Beach BBQ** (Aruba Sonesta Resorts at Seaport Village, L. G. Smith Blvd. 9, Oranjestad, tel. 297/8–36000) on Monday.

It's Tuesday night at the Bon Bini Festival. Performers run onto the stage, while steel-pan drummers pound out a heart-racing beat. The rhythm prompts a local dance troupe to converge on the scene; they mesmerize the audience with their traditional movements and colorful costumes. One observer, an island visitor, gets up and dances. A local man with a bead of sweat on his brow flashes her a bright smile and says, "Hey, you ever seen this before? This is the good stuff."

In this Chapter

the arts

PUERTO RICO HAS RICKY MARTIN, Jamaica has Bob Marley, and
Aruba has . . . well, Aruba has a handful of stars who aren't
quite as famous but are just as talented. Over the years, several
local artists including composer Julio Renado Euson (who once
won a competition against Ricky Martin), choreographer Wilma
Kuiperi, sculptor Ciro Abath, and visual artist Elvis Lopez have
gained international renown. Further, many Aruban musicians
play more than one type of music (classical, jazz, soca, salsa,
reggae, calypso, rap, pop), and many can compose as well as
perform.

The Union of Cultural Organizations (UNOCA) is devoted to
developing local culture while broadening international appeal,
according to director Pancho Geerman. UNOCA provides
scholarships to prepare and enable artists of all ages to
participate in exhibitions, shows, and festivals. Although some
internationally recognized Aruban artists have returned home
to help promote cultural development, Eldin Juddan, president
of the Association of Musicians Arubano (ASOMA) and a
renowned conductor and pianist, says the island needs to be
more interested in local musicians. "There's a lot of talent, but
professional guidance is needed to bring these talents and
music to their potential. They [the professionals] can be
instrumental in leading workshops, giving lectures, and
organizing local performing- and visual-arts events. . . ."

Despite the need for future arts development, several
organizations are currently very active. Both the Mascaruba

Claudius Philips and Oreo

If you're lucky, you might catch Claudius Philips and his 16-member group, Oreo, playing during your island stay. If so, be prepared to wriggle through a crowded dance floor. Claudius—a singer, composer, arranger, and pianist—began performing at age 16. At age 17, he won his first competition during a song festival on St. Maarten. In the past 15 years, he has won the title of "Calypso King" 14 times and "Road March King" 10 times. (A road march is a Carnival song.) He has also been recognized by Aruba's minister of culture for his support of local arts. Claudius and Oreo, which he founded in 1992, perform regularly on Aruba and have also played in Curaçao, Bonaire, St. Maarten, Suriname, Holland, and the United States. Followers are no doubt drawn by the group's versatility; they play everything from calypso, salsa, and meringue to disco. Among the most popular songs are those about island happenings—both political and cultural—as well those that are just plain fun, such as "Saca e Boem Boem" ("Push Out Your Butt").

group and the Foundation for the Arts (FARPA) regularly organize arts projects and shows. The **Cas Di Cultura** (Vondellaan 2, Oranjestad, tel. 297/8–21010), the island's cultural center, continuously hosts art exhibits, folkloric shows, dance performances, and concerts. Further, the island's many festivals showcase arts and culture. To find out what's going on, contact the Cas Di Cultura; check out the local newspaper, *Aruba Today*, or *Calalou*, a Caribbean publication dedicated to the visual arts; or phone the national library, which has a bulletin board of events.

ART GALLERIES

ETERNO GALLERY. Here you'll find local and international artists at work. In addition, be sure to stop by for concerts by classical guitarists, dance performances, visual-arts shows, and plays. *Emanstraat 92, Oranjestad, tel. 297/8–39607.*

GALERIA HARMONIA. The island's largest gallery has changing art exhibits as well as a permanent collection of works by local and international artists. *Zeppenfeldstraat 10, San Nicolas, tel. 297/8–42969.*

GASPARITO RESTAURANT AND ART GALLERY. This exceptional dining spot (☞ Eating Out) features an ongoing exhibition of Aruban artists and offers selected works for sale. *Gasparito 3, Noord, tel. 297/8–67044.*

FESTIVALS
Annual Events

ARUBA MUSIC FESTIVAL. Held the first week in June, this concert series features top jazz, R&B, and contemporary Latin performers.

THE DANDE STROLL. New Year's Eve is a big deal to most, but on Aruba, the festivities—which include a midnight fireworks display—continue through New Year's Day. Groups of musicians, known as Dande, stroll from house to house, singing good-luck greetings for the new year. The best Dande song receives a prize and is sung by islanders during the next 12 months.

INTERNATIONAL DANCE FESTIVAL ARUBA. Each October, dance companies from the Caribbean, the United States, and Europe conduct and participate in workshops, lectures, demonstrations, and exhibitions.

INTERNATIONAL THEATRE FESTIVAL ARUBA. Every other October, theater groups from around the world perform 45- to 70-minute shows at the Cas Di Cultura.

JAZZ AND LATIN MUSIC FESTIVAL. For five nights each June, you can hear authentic jazz and Latin music performed at the outdoor venue next to the Aruba Sonesta Resorts at Seaport

Carnival

Aruba's biggest bash incorporates local traditions with those of Venezuela, Brazil, Holland, and North America. Here, Carnival consists of six weeks of jump-ups (the traditional Caribbean street celebration), competitions, parties, and costumed parades. The celebrations culminate with the Grand Parade held in Oranjestad on the Sunday before Ash Wednesday. It lasts for hours and turns the streets into one big stage. The two main events are the Grand Children's Parade, where children dress in costume and decorate floats, and the Lightening Parade, with miles of glittery floats and lavish costumes. Steel-pan and brass bands supply the music that inspires the crowds to dance. All events end on Shrove Tuesday: at midnight an effigy of King Momo (traditionally depicted as a fat, sympathetic man, who is symbolic of the flesh) is burned, indicating the end of joy and the beginning of Lenten penitence.

Village (☞ Where to Sleep). There's a good deal of dancing in the aisles as well. Tickets and hotel-package information are available from Aruba Tourism Authority offices (☞ Practical Information).

LATIN AMERICAN FILM FESTIVAL. This exhibition of works by Latin American filmmakers usually takes place during the last week in May. Most of the films are in Spanish with English subtitles; some are in English.

NATIONAL ANTHEM AND FLAG DAY. On this official holiday (March 18), you can stop by Plaza Betico Croes in Oranjestad for folkloric presentations and other traditional festivities.

ST. JOHN'S DAY (DERA GAI). This annual "burying of the rooster" festival is celebrated on the Feast of St. John the Baptist (June 24) with festive song, bright yellow and red costumes, and traditional dances at local community centers. The tradition dates from 1862. Today, the rooster—which symbolizes a successful harvest—has been replaced by a *calabash* (gourd).

Weekly Fetes

BON BINI FESTIVAL. This year-round folkloric event is held every Tuesday from 6:30 PM to 8:30 PM at the historic Ft. Zoutman in Oranjestad. Stop by to check out the local arts and crafts, food, drink, music, and dance. The entrance fee is $3.

WATAPANA FOOD AND ART FESTIVAL. Listen to live music, see local art, and indulge in authentic Aruban foods and beverages at the festival grounds between the Hyatt Regency Aruba Beach Resort & Casino and the Allegro Aruba Beach Resort & Casino (☞ Where to Sleep), every Wednesday from 6 PM to 8 PM, from May through October. Admission is free.

A visitor from the States became frustrated when he couldn't get in touch with his family—either via the Internet or his long-distance phone service—from his hotel. Another hotelier overheard the visitor complain about the problem to a beach buddy. The hotelier immediately offered to let the visitor use the facilities at his hotel, handing over a key to the private computer room. And, of course, the hotelier also invited the visitor to join him for coffee.

In this Chapter

where to sleep

"CUIDA NOS TURISTA" (*"TAKE CARE OF OUR TOURISTS"*) is the island's motto, and Arubans are taught the finer points of hospitality as soon as they learn to read and write. With such cordial hosts, it's hard to go wrong no matter which accommodation you choose.

Most hotels are west of Oranjestad, along L. G. Smith and J. E. Irausquin boulevards. Many are self-contained complexes, with water-sports centers, health clubs, restaurants, shops, casinos, and car-rental and travel desks. Room service, laundry and dry-cleaning services, in-room safes and minibars or refrigerators, and baby-sitting services are standard at all but the smallest properties, and many daily activities are usually part of the package. Most properties don't include meals in their rates. Still, you can shop around for good dining options, as hotel restaurants and clubs are open to all island guests.

Many people stay in time-shares, returning year after year and making the island a kind of home away from home. Some time-share patrons say they like the spacious, homey accommodations and the option of preparing their own meals. Note that hotel-type amenities such as shampoo, hair dryers, and housekeeping service may not be offered in time shares; if they are, they often cost extra. Also note that there's a daily occupancy tax of 16.55% (for properties that aren't members of the Aruba Hotel and Tourism Association [AHATA]) or 17.66% (for AHATA members) in lieu of the 6% hotel tax. Be sure to ask about occupancy and hotel taxes before booking.

At press time, plans were in the works to introduce a special program for frequent visitors to Aruba: automatic check-in at the airport (sign in, get your key, and head right to your hotel room). Check with your travel agent to see if the plan has taken effect and whether you qualify. There are, however, a few perks already in place for repeat island visitors: return for 10 consecutive years, and a picture taken of you and a tourist board representative will be published in a local paper; come for 20 years in a row, and you'll be named a good-will ambassador to the island.

Prices

Hotel rates are high; to save money, take advantage of airline and hotel packages, or visit during low season (summer), when rates are discounted by as much as 40%. If you're traveling with kids, ask about discounts; children often stay for free in their parents' room, though there are age cutoffs for this.

CATEGORY	COST*
$$$$	over $325
$$$	$250–$325
$$	$175–$250
$	under $175

All prices are for a standard double room during high season, excluding government taxes and 11% service charge.

$$$$ ARUBA MARRIOTT RESORT AND STELLARIS CASINO. Aruba's
★   most expensive high-rise resort is on the far end of Palm Beach, close to the Tierra del Sol golf course. You'll hear the sound of water everywhere, whether it's the beating of the surf or the trickling of streams and waterfalls in the marble lobby and around the tropically landscaped free-form pool. Spacious rooms have crisp green-on-white decor softened by floral bedspreads and pastel watercolor paintings; most have an ocean view and a spartan balcony, as well as walk-in closets, hair

Associations That Accommodate

The **Aruba Hotel and Tourism Association** (AHATA; tel. 297/8–22607) was established in 1965 to maintain high industry standards. From its original seven hotels, it has grown into a powerhouse of more than 80 members, including restaurants, casinos, stores, tour operators, and airlines.

AHATA's $1 million annual budget, earmarked to promote Aruba as a travel destination, is matched by the government's Aruba Tourism Authority and by private sector partners. It maintains a hot line (via e-mail from Aruba Tourism Web site at www.arubatourism.com) where you can express opinions and register complaints. AHATA is also involved in an island cleanup effort as part of the Aruba Limpi (Aruba Clean) Committee.

Another association, the **Aruba Apartment Resort and Small Hotel Association** (ARASA; tel. 297/8–23289), expressly targets quality control in smaller, less expensive hotels. Members are expected to meet certain standards of accommodations and service and still offer affordable (often as low as $65 per night) rates.

dryers, and irons. The walk to the ocean from the garden-view rooms in the veranda building is longer than that from elsewhere, but the in-room Jacuzzis more than compensate for this. The pricey Tuscany restaurant (☞ Eating Out) offers superlative Italian cuisine, and the Simply Fish eatery seats 35 for dinner. Guests at the Ocean Club (☞ below), an adjacent time-share property, have access to the restaurants and shops in the main resort. L. G. Smith Blvd. 101, Palm Beach, tel. 297/8–69000 or 800/223–6388, fax 297/8–60649. 372 rooms, 41 suites. 4 restaurants, 4 bars, café, air-conditioning, in-room data ports, in-room safes, minibars, no-smoking floors, pool, 2 tennis courts, beauty salon, massage, saunas, spa, aerobics, health club, volleyball, beach, dive shop, windsurfing, boating, jet skiing, shops, casino, concierge, car rental, meeting rooms. AE, D, DC, MC, V. EP, FAP, MAP.

$$$$ COSTA LINDA BEACH RESORT. The name, which means "beautiful coast," speaks for itself. This paradise on earth is on a 183-m (600-ft) stretch of pristine Eagle Beach. A sparkling blue pool sits in the center of the manicured grounds. A blend of Dutch, Spanish, and Portuguese influences is evident in the architecture. Let yourself be pampered by the attentive staff. Be comforted by the numerous amenities in the bright, spacious two- and three-bedroom suites (all with two bathrooms), including Roman tubs, hair dryers, dining tables, sofas, direct-dial phones, two TVs, radios, and balconies overlooking the crystalline sea. The larger units also have an outdoor Jacuzzi and barbecue grill. The fitness center has racquetball and squash courts; there are lighted tennis courts on site; and scuba diving, snorkeling, and boating opportunities are nearby. In the evening, you can head to the resort's nightclub or make the short walk to the Alhambra Casino (☞ Casinos). *J. E. Irausquin Blvd. 59, Eagle Beach, tel. 297/8–38000, fax 297/8–36040. 155 suites. 3 restaurants, 3 bars, air-conditioning, kitchenettes, refrigerators, pool, wading pool, 2 tennis courts, health club, shops, baby-sitting, coin laundry, dry cleaning, children's programs. AE, DC, MC, V. BP, CP, EP, MAP.*

$$$$ HYATT REGENCY ARUBA BEACH RESORT & CASINO. A top
★ choice for honeymooners, this resort looks like a Spanish grandee's palace, with art deco–style flourishes and a multilevel pool with waterfalls, a two-story water slide, and a lagoon stocked with tropical fish and black swans. Rooms, done in gemstone color schemes and dark mahogany furnishings, have tiny balconies and lots of extras; those on the Regency Club floor have such amenities as free Continental breakfast and concierge service. You can relax on the beach, have a game of tennis, or head out for a horseback ride before an afternoon hydrotherapy treatment and a stop at the juice bar. For a full

meal choose from four excellent restaurants: Olé (Spanish); the Palm (contemporary Caribbean); Piccolo (Italian); and Ruinas del Mar (Continental). Families will appreciate Camp Hyatt, which imaginatively incorporates Aruban storytelling, cooking, and arts and crafts for kids ages 3–12. *J. E. Irausquin Blvd. 85, Palm Beach, tel. 297/8–61234 or 800/554–9288, fax 297/8–61682. 342 rooms, 18 suites. 4 restaurants, 5 bars, snack bar, air-conditioning, fans, in-room safes, minibars, no-smoking floor, room service, pool, beauty salon, 2 outdoor hot tubs, massage, sauna, spa, steam rooms, 2 tennis courts, basketball, health club, horseback riding, volleyball, beach, dive shop, dock, snorkeling, water slide, windsurfing, boating, jet skiing, waterskiing, shops, casino, baby-sitting, children's programs, playground, concierge, business services, travel services, car rental. AE, D, DC, MC, V. EP, MAP.*

$$$$ **MARRIOTT ARUBA OCEAN CLUB.** First-rate amenities and
★ lushly decorated villas have made this time share the talk of the island. Each one- and two-bedroom unit counts a spectacular ocean view, a balcony, and a kitchen among its amenities. The S-shape pool, which is constructed of rock, has a swim-up bar and waterfalls; there are four spa Jacuzzis built into the rocks above the pool. As a guest here, you also have access to the facilities at the adjacent Aruba Marriott Resort and Stellaris Casino (☞ *above*), including the pool and spa, the fitness center, and the casino. *L. G. Smith Blvd. 101, Palm Beach, tel. 297/ 8–62641, fax 297/8–68000. 218 units. Restaurant, grocery, kitchenettes, refrigerators, pool, spa, beach, dive shop, snorkeling, boating, jet skiing, windsurfing, shops. AE, D, DC, MC, V. BP, EP.*

$$$$ **TAMARIJN ARUBA ALL INCLUSIVE BEACH RESORT.** Low-rise buildings stretch along the property of this low-key all-inclusive, whose spacious, casual, oceanfront rooms have white-tile floors, light-wood furnishings, painted-tile bathrooms, and patios or balconies. The resort caters to both couples and families (including those from its sister property, the Divi Aruba resort; ☞ *below*), and the package here covers meals, snacks, all

lodging

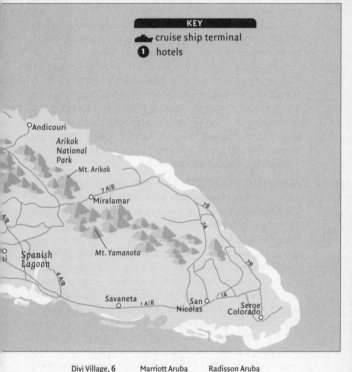

KEY

🚢 cruise ship terminal

❶ hotels

Andicouri

Arikok National Park

Mt. Arikok

7 A|B

Miralamar

7B

7A

Mt. Yamanota

Spanish Lagoon

A|B

4 A|B

7B

Savaneta

1 A|B

San Nicolas

7A

Seroe Colorado

Divi Village, 6

Dutch Village, 7

Holiday Inn Aruba Beach Resort & Casino, 23

Hyatt Regency Aruba Beach Resort & Casino, 19

Manchebo Beach Resort, 11

Marriott Aruba Ocean Club, 17

Mill Resort & Suites, 31

Paradise Beach Villas, 8

Playa Linda Beach Resort, 26

La Quinta Beach Resort, 14

Radisson Aruba Resort, 24

Stauffer Hotel, 27

Tamarijn Aruba All Inclusive Beach Resort, 4

Vistalmar, 33

Wyndham Aruba Beach Resort and Casino, 21

beverages, entertainment, tickets to the Bon Bini Festival (☞ Arts), and an array of outdoor activities. A bar at one end of the property serves food and drinks as a convenience for guests more removed from the main restaurants. Other conveniences include a free hourly ('til 3 AM) shuttle to the Alhambra Casino. At press time, a face-lift for the lobby and other projects were in the works. *J. E. Irausquin Blvd. 41, Punta Brabo, tel. 297/8–24150 or 800/554–2008, fax 297/8–31940. 236 rooms. 3 restaurants, 2 bars, snack bar, air-conditioning, fans, 2 pools, 2 tennis courts, health club, Ping-Pong, shuffleboard, volleyball, beach, snorkeling, windsurfing, boating, waterskiing, fishing, bicycles, shops, car rental. AE, D, DC, MC, V. All-inclusive. www.tamarijnaruba.com*

$$$–$$$$ ALLEGRO ARUBA RESORT & CASINO. Activity surrounds the cloverleaf-shape pool (with its waterfall and whirlpool tubs) at the heart of this resort. It's a popular place with tour groups (there are plans to renovate the lobby to accommodate long check-in lines), and the buzzing atmosphere includes everything from beer-drinking contests to bikini shows. In rooms the white-tile bathrooms are tight, and the balconies are narrow step-outs, but recent improvements include tropical-decor touches and better air-conditioning. The Kids' Club, open from 9 to 5 daily, is for ages 4–12. *J. E. Irausquin Blvd. 83, Palm Beach, tel. 297/8–64500 or 800/447–7462, fax 297/8–63191. 405 rooms, 14 suites. 3 restaurants, 4 bars, air-conditioning, in-room safes, pool, 2 outdoor hot tubs, 2 tennis courts, basketball, exercise room, Ping-Pong, volleyball, beach, snorkeling, boating, waterskiing, shops, casino, dance club, children's programs. AE, D, DC, MC, V. All-inclusive, EP.*

$$$–$$$$ ARUBA SONESTA RESORTS AT SEAPORT VILLAGE. For those
★ who enjoy being in the thick of things (like Queen Beatrix, who stayed here in the fall of 1999), this lively Oranjestad property is surrounded by shops, restaurants, and casinos. It's a top choice for singles, yet it also has plenty for families (though if you need

time away from the kids, take advantage of the island's nanny program). Senior citizens appreciate the discounted room rates they receive. The newer building—whose roomy Sonesta Suites have kitchenettes and ceiling fans—is near a private man-made beach. The original high-rise hotel has compact but attractive rooms; choose the quieter garden-view rooms here. In the lobby, which is connected to the Seaport Village Mall, you can board a skiff for a day trip along a canal to the resort's 40-acre private island. The gourmet restaurant, L'Escale (☞ Eating Out), is one of Aruba's best. *L. G. Smith Blvd. 9, Oranjestad, tel. 297/8–36000 or 800/766–3782, fax 297/8–25317. 285 rooms, 265 suites. 4 restaurants, 5 bars, air-conditioning, kitchenettes (some), minibars, no-smoking rooms, room service, 3 pools, massage, golf privileges, tennis court, exercise room, volleyball, beach, dive shop, snorkeling, jet skiing, marina, water skiing, fishing, shops, 2 casinos, nightclub, children's programs, playground, coin laundry, concierge, convention center. AE, D, DC, MC, V. All-inclusive, EP, FAP, MAP. www.arubasonesta.com*

$$$–$$$$ DIVI ARUBA BEACH RESORT MEGA ALL INCLUSIVE. At this Mediterranean-style resort you can choose from standard guest rooms, beachfront lanai rooms, and *casitas* that look out onto courtyards and are, for the most part, only steps from the beach. The white-tile floors, light-wood furniture, and mint and jade color schemes are soothing. Drop by the make-your-own daiquiri station at the poolside Pelican Bar, which also has a pizza oven. In addition to the many on-site facilities, you can also use those at the adjacent Tamarijn Aruba (☞ *above*). Note that despite the "mega all-inclusive" label, getting your laundry done, having your hair cut, or hiring a baby-sitter costs extra. *L. G. Smith Blvd. 93, Manchebo Beach, tel. 297/8–23300 or 800/554–2008, fax 297/8–31940. 203 rooms. 5 restaurants, 3 bars, air-conditioning, fans, refrigerators, 2 pools, beauty salon, outdoor hot tub, tennis court, exercise room, shuffleboard, volleyball, beach, dive shop, snorkeling,* *windsurfing, boating, waterskiing, bicycles, shops, baby-sitting, laundry service. AE, D, DC, MC, V. All-inclusive. www.diviaruba.com*

$$$–$$$$ **PLAYA LINDA BEACH RESORT.** It's hard to tell the difference between dream and reality at this luscious resort, which is shaped like a pyramid. Set right on a sandy white beach, the luxurious studios and one- and two-bedroom suites are spacious, beautifully designed, and lavishly decorated. By day, frolic on the beach, take a dip in the free-form pool or one of the Jacuzzis, have a game of tennis, or shop in the arcade. After dining in one of the restaurants or preparing a meal in your fully equipped kitchen, shun the radio and satellite TV in favor of the sea view from the large terrace. Other evening entertainment options include the free weekly manager's cocktail party. *J. E. Irausquin Blvd. 87, Palm Beach, tel. 297/8–61000, fax 297/8–65210. 194 units. 2 restaurants, 3 bars, air-conditioning, in-room safes, kitchenettes, refrigerators, pool, 2 hot tubs, putting green, 3 tennis courts, health club, beach, dive shop, windsurfing, boating, fishing, shops, baby-sitting, coin laundry. AE, D, DC, V. CP. www.playalinda.com*

$$$–$$$$ **RADISSON ARUBA CARIBBEAN RESORT.** Aruba's newest and
★ largest hotel stretches out over 14 acres. It reopened at the start of this century (after a $59 million transformation), with promises to pamper and indulge its guests. If you're early for check-in, get comfortable in the courtesy suites, which have lockers, changing rooms, and showers. The colonial Caribbean–style guest rooms (each with an ocean, partial ocean, or garden view) feature mahogany four-poster beds and such singular accents as hand-beaded lamp shades or unique metal ashtrays. The designers have thought of everything: blue accent lighting, wood furniture on the balconies, and plantation shutters. Other in-room perks include minibars (your first bottle of Evian is free), coffeemakers, makeup mirrors, and hair dryers. Unwind in the fitness center and spa, and then enjoy a meal at one of the hotel's excellent restaurants. *J. E. Irausquin Boulevard 81, Palm Beach, tel. 297/8–66555, fax 297/8–63260. 358 rooms, 32 suites. 4*

restaurants, 3 bars, air-conditioning, in-room data ports, in-room safes, minibars, room service, 2 pools, spa, 2 tennis courts, golf privileges, health club, beach, dive shop, snorkeling, boating, jet skiing, baby-sitting, children's programs, dry cleaning, laundry service, business services, convention center, meeting rooms. AE, D, DC, MC, V. BP, FAP, MAP. www.radisson.com

$$$–$$$$ **WYNDHAM ARUBA BEACH RESORT AND CASINO.** If bustle and nonstop activity make your day, you'll be right at home here. The grand public areas are cavernous enough to accommodate big groups from North and South America, which make up a good portion of the clientele. Rooms, which are average in size and oddly configured, have gold, khaki, and blue bedspreads; mustard-color stucco walls; and handsome dark-wood furniture. All have ocean-view balconies and are equipped with coffeemakers, irons, refrigerators, and hair dryers. A day at the pool means more than swimming and sunning; a "pool concierge" makes the rounds, providing books, magazines, CDs, and CD players that you can borrow for the day; pool attendants spritz you with Evian, offer chilled towels, and serve frozen drinks. If you still don't feel pampered, head to the health club for a massage, a facial, or a sauna. J. E. Irausquin Blvd. 77, Palm Beach, tel. 297/8–64466 or 800/996–3426, fax 297/8–68217. 478 rooms, 78 suites. 4 restaurants, 5 bars, air-conditioning, in-room safes, pool, wading pool, beauty salon, massage, sauna, steam room, tennis court, health club, Ping-Pong, shuffleboard, volleyball, beach, dive shop, snorkeling, windsurfing, boating, jet skiing, parasailing, waterskiing, shops, casino, concierge, convention center. AE, D, DC, MC, V. All-inclusive, CP, EP, FAP, MAP.

$$–$$$$ **CASA DEL MAR BEACH RESORT.** This beachside resort across from the Alhambra Casino (☞ Casinos) offers two parts recreation, one part rest and relaxation. Whether you stay in the main wing's two-bedroom Presidential Suites or the one-bedroom Ambassador Wing suites, the accommodations are deluxe and comfortable. Balconies or terraces, TVs, and fully equipped

kitchens are among the amenities. Play tennis on one of four lighted courts, work out in the exercise room, take an aquacize class in the pool, arrange for water sports or tours at the activities desk, or kick back with a book or game from the library. Fiesta at the daily happy hours and at the Wednesday-night member's cocktail party, and dine on fine Italian cuisine at the waterfront La Gondola at the Seagull Restaurant. Kids ages 4–10 will enjoy the special programs weekdays 10–noon; on Tuesday all the young ones are invited to the 6 PM pizza party ($10 per child). *L. G. Smith Boulevard 51–53, Manchebo Beach, tel. 297/8–23000 or 297/8–27000, fax 297/8–38191. 147 suites. Restaurant, bar, grocery, air-conditioning, in-room safes, kitchenettes, refrigerators, 2 pools, wading pool, beauty salon, hot tub, 4 tennis courts, beach, shops, library, children's programs, coin laundry, travel services, car rental. AE, D, DC, MC, V. EP.*

$$–$$$ **ARUBA GRAND BEACH RESORT & CASINO.** Although this privately owned eight-story property underwent extensive renovations in 1998–99, some things never change: the atmosphere remains low-key, and the repeat business is still high. The once pink building is now yellow and white to complement a jade green roof; at press time, 55 thatched-roof beach huts and a spa were in the works. The large rooms and suites have new furniture, bedding, and such amenities as large walk-in closets and balconies that overlook either the ocean, the pool, or the garden. The Seawatch restaurant offers international cuisine for breakfast, lunch, and dinner; the Whale's Rib entices guests seeking seafood fare in a more casual setting. Ask about packages; discounts are available for children under 12. *J. E. Irausquin Blvd. 79, Palm Beach, tel. 297/8–63900 or 800/345–2782, fax 297/8–61941. 130 rooms, 41 suites. 2 restaurants, 3 bars, deli, ice cream parlor, air-conditioning, in-room safes, refrigerators, room service, pool, wading pool, 2 tennis courts, volleyball, beach, dive shop, snorkeling, windsurfing, boating, waterskiing, shops, casino, baby-sitting, dry cleaning, laundry service, concierge, meeting rooms. AE, D, DC, MC, V. All-inclusive, EP, MAP.*

$$–$$$ ★ BUCUTI BEACH RESORT. Owner Ewald Biemans must be doing something right; he recently won the AHATA's hotelier of the year award. His intimate European-style resort is refreshingly peaceful. Popular with honeymooners (their doorways are charmingly decorated), the hacienda-style buildings house enormous, sunny rooms that have tropical decor, handsome cherrywood furnishings, sparkling tile floors, and a terrace or balcony with an ocean view. Room extras include coffeemakers, microwaves, hair dryers, irons, bins for recyclables, and devices for people with hearing impairments. The grounds are lushly landscaped, and the resort has an enviable location on the widest, most secluded section of Eagle Beach. The oceanfront Pirate's Nest restaurant looks like a beached galleon and is known for its dinners of lobster-size shrimp and expansive salad bar. If you feel like working off calories, head for the open-air exercise pavilion. Need to stay connected to the real world? The hotel has a 24-hour business center with computers and Internet access. *L. G. Smith Blvd. 55-B (Box 1299), Eagle Beach, tel. 297/8–31100 or 800/223–1108, fax 297/8–25272. 58 rooms, 5 suites. Restaurant, bar, grocery, air-conditioning, fans, in-room safes, minibars, refrigerators, pool, beach, bicycles, shop, coin laundry, travel services, business services. AE, D, DC, MC, V. CP, MAP.*

$$–$$$ HOLIDAY INN ARUBA BEACH RESORT & CASINO. Here, three seven-story buildings are set apart from each other along a sugary, palm-dotted beach. Rooms are clean, spacious, and attractive in shades of green, royal blue, yellow, and orange. The pool's cascades and sundeck draw as large a crowd as the wide beach, where such activities as the Monday-evening managers' cocktail party take place. As many as two children can stay with their parents at no extra charge, and the resort has a free Little Rascals Club for kids 5–12. Enjoy live entertainment as you try your luck at the casino, or savor a beachfront meal at the Sea Breeze Grill. Look for a new spa (being planned at press time) with massages, wraps, and facials. *J. E. Irausquin Blvd. 230, Palm*

Beach, tel. 297/8–60236, 800/934–6750 (direct to hotel), fax 297/8–60323. 600 rooms, 15 suites. 3 restaurants, 3 bars, air-conditioning, no-smoking rooms, refrigerators, 2 pools, massage, 4 tennis courts, basketball, exercise room, Ping-Pong, volleyball, beach, dive shop, dock, snorkeling, windsurfing, boating, waterskiing, shops, casino, children's programs, concierge, meeting rooms. AE, DC, MC, V. All-inclusive, EP, FAP, MAP.

$$ AMSTERDAM MANOR BEACH RESORT. This mustard-color hotel—all gables and turrets—looks like part of a Dutch colonial village. It's a cozy enclave that surrounds a pool with a waterfall, and glorious Eagle Beach is just across the street. Rooms are furnished in either Dutch modern or provincial style and range from small studios—some with a balcony and/or a whirlpool tub—to two-bedroom suites with peaked ceilings, whirlpool tubs and showers, and full kitchens. Up to two children under 12 stay free with their parents. Free diving lessons are available twice a week, and the hotel can arrange a variety of activities. J. E. Irausquin Blvd. 252, Eagle Beach, tel. 297/8–71492 or 800/766–6016 (direct to hotel), fax 297/8–71463. 70 units. Restaurant, bar, air-conditioning, fans, in-room safes, kitchenettes, pool, wading pool, snorkeling, playground, coin laundry, car rental. AE, DC, MC, V. CP, EP, MAP.

$$ ARUBA BEACH CLUB. Colonial charm coupled with Dutch hospitality creates an ambience that keeps people returning. All studios and one-bedroom units in this time-share property have bamboo furniture, off-white walls, and printed curtains; amenities include satellite TV and a balcony or a terrace—sometimes with an ocean view. There's plenty to do on site, including yoga and Papiamento classes. The staff at the tour desk can arrange for water sports and other activities. Kids will enjoy the playground as well as their own pool. A shopping arcade includes boutiques, a frozen yogurt shop, and a cybercafé; if these amenities aren't enough, a stay here also enables you to use the facilities at the adjoining Casa del Mar

Rest Easy

Even the softest of sheets can feel scratchy against sun-burnt skin. Before bed, try a local product made with the aloe vera plant—an Aruban treasure that's been cultivated here since the 1840s. The gel from inside the plant's fibrous, water-retaining leaves is the key skin-moisturizing ingredient in **Aruba Aloe Balm**'s (tel. 800/95–ARUBA, arubaaloe.com) Burn Balm, a great after-sun soother. The company also puts aloe in everything from lipstick to soap to hair spray.

If a pre-bed application of an aloe product doesn't soothe your sun-kissed skin and traveler's soul, perhaps a local sleeplessness remedy will. The rest of the world may resort to counting sheep, but Aruban insomniacs turn to basil. Babies who can't settle in are given an herbal tea made from the tops of the white basil plant, which grows readily on the island. If your valerian root doesn't do the trick, a more potent version of this tea just might. Bon nochi.

Beach Resort (☞ above). J. E. Irausquin Blvd. 53, Manchebo Beach, tel. 297/8–23000, fax 297/8–26557. 89 rooms, 42 suites. Restaurant, bar, café, grocery, air-conditioning, kitchenettes, in-room safes, pool, wading pool, beauty salon, 2 tennis courts, health club, shops, baby-sitting, children's programs, playground, laundry service, travel services, car rental. AE, D, DC, MC, V. EP. www.arubabeachclub.com

$$ ARUBA PHOENIX BEACH RESORT. A breathtaking location, a plethora of amenities, and a lively atmosphere make the Phoenix popular. In many of the studio and one- or two-bedroom units, a balcony or patio affords ocean views. Light-wood furnishings, tropical color schemes, and lots of plants help to make you feel at home. Coffeemakers, microwaves, alarm-clock radios, irons, hair dryers, and satellite TV are among the thoughtful touches, and some rooms are wheelchair accessible. In the evenings, enjoy live entertainment and theme events, mingle with other guests at the weekly manager's cocktail party, or try your luck at the nearby Alhambra Casino (☞ Casinos). *J. E. Irausquin Blvd. 75, Palm Beach, tel. 297/8–61170, fax 297/8–61165. 101 units. Restaurant, bar, deli, grocery, air-conditioning, fans, kitchenettes, in-room safes, in-room VCRs, refrigerators, 2 pools, hot tub, beach, snorkeling, health club, volleyball, boating, children's programs, meeting rooms, travel services. AE, D, DC, MC, V. EP.*

$$ BOARDWALK VACATION RETREAT. The owners describe this small retreat as offering "far-from-it-all tranquillity with close-to-it-all convenience." The suites are in casitas enveloped by gardens, replete with exotic palms, hummingbirds, and butterflies. Yet a stay here puts you only a few yards from the beach and within walking distance of casinos and water-sports facilities. Each unit has comfortable rattan furnishings, tropical fabrics, white-tile floors, a large living room, a kitchen, and a patio with a barbecue and hammocks. Housekeeping service is provided every other day. Laundry service is also available. The facility caters to windsurfers; at the catered Caribbean dinner party each Thursday, you can watch (and buy) videos of the day's activity on the water. *Bakval 20, Palm Beach, tel. 297/8–66654, fax 297/8–61836. 13 units. Grocery, air-conditioning, in-room VCRs, kitchenettes, refrigerators, pool, wading pool, hot tub, baby-sitting. AE, MC, V. EP. www.theboardwalk-aruba.com*

$$ LA CABANA ALL SUITE BEACH RESORT & CASINO. Across the street from Eagle Beach is this self-contained, well-maintained resort village. The original four-story building faces the beach and forms a horseshoe around a huge free-form pool with a water slide, a bar, a restaurant, and a water-sports center. One-third of the studio and one-bedroom suites have full sea views. All have kitchenettes, balconies, and Jacuzzis. Pricier suites and villas are separated from the main building by a parking lot, making them more secluded. The Home Food Shopping Program here means someone else does the work (for a $5 fee) during your stay or even before you check in. You can order groceries on-line (www.lacabana.com/groceries) up to two days prior to travel, and they'll be delivered upon your arrival. Deliveries are made once a day between 10 AM and 11 AM. J. E. Irausquin Blvd. 250, Eagle Beach, tel. 297/8–79000, 212/251–1710 in NY, or 800/835–7193; fax 297/8–70834. 803 suites. 4 restaurants, 3 bars, grocery, ice cream parlor, air-conditioning, in-room safes, kitchenettes, 3 pools, 3 outdoor hot tubs, massage, sauna, 5 tennis courts, aerobics, basketball, health club, racquetball, shuffleboard, squash, volleyball, water slide, dive shop. AE, DC, MC, V. All-inclusive, EP, FAP, MAP.

$$ DIVI VILLAGE. A lush, tropical feel pervades this self-contained time-share resort across the street from the beach. Accommodations range from multilevel efficiencies to apartments to penthouses. Balconies or patios, air-conditioning, satellite TV, and full kitchens are among the amenities. Enjoy tennis on site and water-sports facilities, shops, restaurants, and clubs at the adjacent Divi Aruba, Dutch Village, and Tamarijn Aruba resorts (☞ above and below). The Alhambra Casino (☞ Casinos) is also nearby. J. E. Irausquin Blvd. 47, Punta Brabo, tel. 297/8–23300 or 800/367–3484, fax 297/8–20501. 153 units. Restaurant, bar, air-conditioning, kitchenettes, refrigerators, tennis court. AE, DC, MC, V. EP.

$$ MANCHEBO BEACH RESORT. This resort has "location, location, location." It's set on one of the prettiest stretches of Eagle Beach amid 100 acres of gardens with everything from bougainvillea to cacti. Manchebo is also just five minutes from town and right across from the Alhambra complex of shops, restaurants, and a casino. The atmosphere is mellow, with an international clientele that appreciates a bargain (children under 12 stay free with their parents). Rooms are of a good size, decorated with blond-wood furnishings and bright floral fabrics and equipped with such comforts as Simmons mattresses and coffeemakers. The French Steakhouse is renowned for its *churrasco* (Argentine mixed grill) and draws diners from all over the island. The beachfront chapel is a charming spot for weddings. *J. E. Irausquin Blvd. 55, Eagle Beach, tel. 297/8–23444 or 800/528–1234, fax 297/8–33667 or 297/8–32446. 71 rooms. 2 restaurants, 2 bars, snack bar, air-conditioning, fans, in-room safes, refrigerators, pool, beach, dive shop, snorkeling, shops, chapel, car rental. AE, D, DC, MC, V. EP, MAP.*

$$ LA QUINTA BEACH RESORT. The atmosphere at this time-share complex is quiet and relaxed. The air-conditioned one-, two-, and three-bedroom apartments have living-dining areas and kitchenettes; daily housekeeping service is a real perk. All the suites have terraces or balconies with garden or ocean views. The resort is adjacent to the Alhambra Casino (☞ Casinos) and across the street from the beach, where you can participate in water sports. Mingle with other guests at the poolside bar or the Thursday-night barbecue. *L. G. Smith Blvd. 228, Eagle Beach, tel. 297/8–75010, fax 297/8–76263. 54 units. 2 restaurants, bar, grocery, air-conditioning, kitchenettes, refrigerators, 2 pools, outdoor hot tub, tennis court, nightclub, baby-sitting, laundry service, car rental. AE, MC, V. EP.*

$-$$ BUSHIRI BEACH RESORT. A small, sandy cove 20 minutes on foot from Oranjestad is the setting for this low-rise, value-oriented all-inclusive. Although the atmosphere is low-key, there's plenty to do, with Papiamento or arts-and-crafts classes, tennis clinics, scuba diving and windsurfing opportunities, and nightly entertainment. The Italian restaurant serves dinner; another, more casual restaurant offers a breakfast buffet and lunch. In addition to food, beverages, and activities, airport transfers, taxes, and tips are included in the room rate. *L. G. Smith Blvd. 35, Punta Brabo, tel. 297/8–25216, fax 297/8–26789. 150 rooms, 4 suites. 2 restaurants, bar, air-conditioning, fans, pool, wading pool, 3 hot tubs, 2 tennis courts, health club, beach, dive shop,* snorkeling, windsurfing, boating, shops, baby-sitting, children's programs, laundry service, travel services, car rental. AE, D, DC, MC, V. All-inclusive.

$–$$ MILL RESORT & SUITES. This small, award-winning resort's whitewashed, red-roof buildings flank its open-air common areas. The architecture is striking: clean geometric lines, skylights, and wood-beam ceilings. The rooms are appealing, with blond-wood and rattan furnishings and a cool powder-blue color scheme. Junior suites have a king-size bed, a sitting area, and a kitchenette. Studios have a full kitchen, a convertible sofa bed or twin beds, a tiny bathroom, and no balcony. The beach is only a five-minute walk away; a morning coffee hour and a weekly scuba lesson are among the on-site amenities. At the Garden Cafe a special tourist menu offers three courses at affordable prices. *J. E. Irausquin Blvd. 330, Oranjestad, tel. 297/8–67700, fax 297/8–67271. 64 studios, 128 suites. Restaurant, bar, grill, grocery, air-conditioning, in-room safes, kitchenettes, 2 pools, wading pool, beauty salon, massage, saunas, 2 tennis courts, exercise room, shops, coin laundry, travel services, car rental. AE, D, DC, MC, V. EP. www.millresort.com*

$ ARUBA MILLENNIUM RESORT. Renovated to usher in the new millennium, this low-key complex is only a two-minute walk from Palm Beach. The studio and one-bedroom apartments now have sleek modern furnishings, fresh coats of white paint, white-tile floors, and floral-print fabrics in subdued blues and yellows. In-room amenities include full, well-equipped kitchens; dining rooms; and balconies. Dip into one of the four whirlpools right outside the suites, seek refreshment at the poolside bar, and catch up on your reading on the sundeck. Six casinos and many fine restaurants are within walking distance. For longer stays, inquire about the resort's weekly and monthly rates. *Palm Beach Rd. 33, Palm Beach, tel. 297/8–61120, fax 297/8–62506. 32 units. Bar, air-conditioning, fans, kitchenettes, refrigerators, pool, 4 outdoor hot tubs. AE, MC, V. EP. www.arubamillenniumresort.com*

$ CARIBBEAN PALM VILLAGE. Lush gardens lend an air of tranquillity to this low-rise resort 1 mi from Palm Beach. The one- or two-bedroom suites have balconies, king- or queen-size beds, direct-dial phones, satellite TVs, and fully equipped kitchens. The Coco Loco Pool Bar serves up breakfast, lunch, and cocktails; after enjoying some food, you can serve up aces on the tennis court. A do-it-yourself dinner made in the barbecue area is a rustic alternative to the romantic Valentino's Italian restaurant. The hotel generally attracts professionals over 30 years old and is a short walk from casinos, nightclubs, water sports, and other attractions. A supermarket, shopping center, and doctor's office are also just moments away. Although Eagle Beach is only a 10-minute walk away, the resort provides daily transportation to and from this sandy stretch; buses depart at 9:30 AM and 12:30 PM and return at 12:30 PM and 4:30 PM. *Palm Beach Rd., Noord 43E, Noord, tel. 297/8–62700, fax 297/8–62380. 170 suites. Restaurant, bar, air-conditioning, fans, kitchenettes, refrigerators, 2 pools, tennis court, hot tub, baby-sitting, car rental. AE, DC, MC, V. EP.*

$ CARIBBEAN TOWN BEACH RESORT. A palm-lined courtyard—complete with a pool, a hot tub, and an open-air bar-restaurant—adorns this cozy property, which attracts a young crowd. All rooms have phones, cable TV, and kitchenettes; some are accessible to people with disabilities. Blue and pink bedspreads nicely complement the white and yellow paint schemes. A stay here gets you free admission to the Havana nightclub (☞ Nightlife) as well as access to the private Havana Beach Club (across the street), which has a dive shop and a bar and grill. Stop by the nightly happy hour, and don't forget: everyone's welcome at the manager's weekly cocktail party. *L. G. Smith Blvd. 2, Oranjestad, tel. 297/8–23380 or 800/223–1108, fax 297/8–32446. 63 rooms. Restaurant, bar, air-conditioning, in-room safes, kitchenettes, refrigerators, 2 pools, hot tub, laundry service, meeting rooms. AE, MC, V. BP, MAP. www.visitaruba.com/caribbeantown*

$ COCONUT INN. Set amid coconut palms in the Aruban countryside, this budget motel offers studios or one-bedroom suites with TVs, direct-dial phones, and full kitchens. The mahogany headboards seem right at home amid the tropical color schemes, which include spreads and draperies with touches of turquoise. Although it's not on the beach, the motel has a pool and a sundeck with cabanas; the island's finest sandy stretches and the major casinos are only a 3-minute drive or a 20-minute walk away. It's a short walk to the public bus stop and to other conveniences, such as a supermarket, a pharmacy, banks, and restaurants. *Noord 31, Noord, tel. 297/8–66288, fax 297/8–65433. 40 units. Restaurant, bar, air-conditioning, kitchenettes, refrigerators, pool, laundry service. MC, V. BP.*

$ DUTCH VILLAGE. Enjoy Old World ambience while basking in New World comforts at this oceanfront time-share complex. It's set around two free-form freshwater pools. Accommodations have Spanish colonial decor, with many hand-crafted accents, as well as private patios, Jacuzzis, kitchens, and satellite TVs. You can participate in various activities and dine in one of several restaurants at the adjoining Divi Aruba, Divi Village, and Tamarijn Aruba resorts (☞ *above*). Steps away, the Alhambra Casino (☞ Casinos) offers shopping and gambling. *J. E. Irausquin Blvd. 47, Punta Brabo, tel. 297/8–23300 or 800/376–3484, fax 297/8–20501. 97 units. Kitchenettes, refrigerators, 2 pools, hot tubs, beach. AE, DC, MC, V. EP.*

$ PARADISE BEACH VILLAS. Decorated in florals and painted in shades of peach, the air-conditioned suites (some of them accessible to people with disabilities) have living rooms, spacious bedrooms, fully equipped kitchens, Jacuzzis, and large balconies with pool or ocean views (in all but four rooms). This low-rise resort attracts many perennial visitors—a sophisticated set generally over age 30. Splash around at one of the two large pools, or mellow out with a dip in an outdoor whirlpool. Let the stress go with a strawberry daiquiri at the poolside bar. If you

Baca Malucu–A Lullaby

This quirky little lullaby has been passed down from generation to generation on Aruba. Once they hear it, children generally go right to sleep ... out of fear.

Papiamento:
Riba Cero di Biento,
Ting Un Baca Malucu,
Muchanan Cu Ta Yora,
Baca Ta Bin Come Nan.

English:
On the windy mountain,
There is a cranky cow,
And when kids cry,
The cow comes and eats them.

need a little more action, you can arrange to participate in water sports—from banana boat rides to jet-skiing jaunts—at the beach near the hotel. On-site conveniences include a drugstore and a mini-mart. *L. G. Smith Blvd., Eagle Beach, tel. 297/8–74000, fax 297/8–70071. 80 units. Restaurant, bar, grocery, air-conditioning, kitchenettes, refrigerators, 2 pools, hot tub, exercise room, beach, shops. AE, D, MC, V. EP.*

$ STAUFFER HOTEL. This economical choice has no grand sea view or sparkling pool, but it is well situated across the street from the high-rise hotels of Palm Beach and within 10 minutes' walk of the main shopping areas. The nearby bus stop makes a rental car unnecessary unless you want to explore farther afield. *J. E. Irausquin Blvd. 370, Palm Beach, tel. 297/8–60855, fax 297/8–*

60856. 100 rooms. Bar, air-conditioning, in-room safes, baby-sitting, coin laundry, car rental. AE, D, DC, MC, V. EP.

$ VISTALMAR. There's no beach here, but the sea and a swimming pier are just across the street. The simply furnished one-bedroom apartments each have a full kitchen, a living-dining room, and a broad sunporch. The friendly owners, Alby and Katy Yarzagaray, provide snorkel gear and stock the refrigerator with breakfast fixings. A drawback is the distance from town, but a rental car can be provided at a reasonable cost, or you can ride the bus ($1.25) that departs from the hotel every two hours. *Bucutiweg 28, south of Oranjestad, tel. 297/8–28579, fax 297/8–22200. 8 rooms. Air-conditioning, kitchenettes, coin laundry, car rental. No credit cards. CP.*

PRACTICAL INFORMATION

Addresses

"Informal" might best describe Aruban addresses. Sometimes the street designation is in English (as in J. E. Irausquin Blvd.), other times in Dutch (as in Wilhelminastraat); sometimes it's not specified whether something is a boulevard or a *straat* (street) at all. Street numbers tend to follow street names, and postal codes aren't used. In rural areas, you might have to ask a local for directions—and be prepared for such instructions as "Take a right at the market, then a left where you see the big divi-divi tree."

Air Travel

Flights arrive daily on Aruba from New York area airports and Miami International Airport, with easy connections from most American cities. Flights are also offered (sometimes via Curaçao) from other American cities, including Atlanta, Baltimore, Houston, Philadelphia, and Tampa. Some airlines fly to the island via San Juan, Puerto Rico.

BOOKING YOUR FLIGHT

When you book **look for nonstop flights** and **remember that "direct" flights stop at least once.** Try to avoid connecting flights, which require a change of plane.

CARRIERS

Air ALM flies daily from Miami via Curaçao; twice a week nonstop from Atlanta; and twice a week from San Juan, Puerto Rico, through Curaçao. The airline also has connecting flights to Caracas, Bonaire, Curaçao, St. Maarten, and other islands, and it offers the Visit Caribbean Pass for interisland travel. Air Aruba flies nonstop daily from Miami and Newark (twice daily on weekends from Newark). There are flights Thursday, Saturday, and Sunday from Tampa and Friday through Monday from

Baltimore and Philadelphia. Air Aruba offers connecting flights to Caracas, Bonaire, Curaçao, St. Maarten, and other islands, and it has a mileage partnership with Continental.

American Airlines offers daily nonstop service from New York and twice daily from San Juan. From Toronto and Montréal the flights are via San Juan. Continental Airlines has nonstop service twice a week from Houston. Delta flies nonstop daily from Atlanta. KLM offers regular service from Amsterdam. TWA has flights daily from San Juan.

➤ **AIRLINES & CONTACTS:** **Air ALM** (tel. 297/8–23546 on Aruba or 800/327–7230 in North America). **Air Aruba** (tel. 297/8–23151 on Aruba or 800/858–8028 in North America). **American Airlines** (tel. 297/8–22700 on Aruba or 800/433–7300 in North America). **Continental Airlines** (tel. 800/525–0280 in North America). **Delta** (tel. 297/8–80044 on Aruba or 800/241–4141 in North America). **KLM** (tel. 297/8–23546 on Aruba or 31/20–4–747–747 in Amsterdam). **TWA** (tel. 800/221–2000 in North America).

CHECK-IN & BOARDING

Checking in, paying departure taxes (if they aren't included in your ticket), clearing security, and boarding can take time. Especially when heading home, **get to the airport at least 1½ hours ahead of time.**

Assuming that not everyone with a ticket will show up, airlines routinely overbook planes. When everyone does, airlines ask for volunteers to give up their seats. In return, these volunteers usually get a certificate for a free flight and are rebooked on the next flight out. If there are not enough volunteers, the airline must choose who will be denied boarding. The first to get bumped are passengers who checked in late and those flying on discounted tickets, so **get to the gate and check in as early as possible,** especially during peak periods.

Always **bring a government-issued photo I.D. to the airport.** You may be asked to show it before you are allowed to check in.

FLYING TIMES

Aruba is 2½ hours from Miami, 4½ hours from New York, and 9½ hours from Amsterdam. The flight from New York to San Juan, Puerto Rico, takes 3½ hours; from Miami to San Juan it's 1½ hours; and from San Juan to Aruba it's just over an hour. Shorter still is the ¼- to ½-hour hop (depending on whether you take a prop or a jet plane) from Curaçao to Aruba.

RECONFIRMING

Be sure to **reconfirm your flights on interisland carriers.** You may be subject to a small carrier's whims: if no other passengers are booked on your flight, you may be requested (actually, ordered) to take a more convenient departure for the airline, or your plane may make unscheduled stops to pick up more clients or cargo. It's all part of the excitement—and unpredictability— of Caribbean travel. In addition, small regional carriers usually have weight restrictions; **travel light,** or you could be subject to outrageous surcharges or delays in getting very large or heavy luggage, which may have to follow on another flight.

Airport & Transfers

AIRPORT

At press time Aruba's Aeropuerto Internacional Reina Beatrix (Queen Beatrix International Airport), just inland from the middle of the south coast, was undergoing an expansion and renovations to transform it into a modern, passenger-friendly facility. Look for new concession areas, business lounges, escalators, elevators, rest rooms, covered walkways, and baggage claim areas, and the all-new Rover Room (intelligence department).

➤ AIRPORT INFORMATION: **Aeropuerto Internacional Reina Beatrix** (tel. 297/8–24800).

TRANSFERS

A taxi from the airport to most hotels takes about 20 minutes. It will cost about $16 to get to Eagle Beach; $18 to the high-rise hotels on Palm Beach; and $9 to the hotels downtown. You'll find a taxi stand right outside the baggage claim area.

Business Hours

Bank hours are weekdays 8:15–5:45; some close from noon to 1 (the Caribbean Mercantile Bank at the airport is open Saturday 9–4 and Sunday 9–1). The central post office in Oranjestad is catercorner from the San Francisco Church and is open weekdays 7:30–noon and 1–4:30. The post office in the Royal Plaza Mall is open Monday–Saturday 7 AM–6:45 PM. Shops are generally open Monday–Saturday 8:30–6. Some stores stay open through the lunch hour, noon–2, and many open when cruise ships are in port on Sunday and holidays.

Bus Travel

Each day (from 6 AM to midnight) buses make hourly trips between the beach hotels and Oranjestad. The one-way fare is Afl2 or US$1.15 (round trip is Afl3.50 or US$2), and exact change is preferred. Buses also run down the coast from Oranjestad to San Nicolas for the same fare. Contact the Aruba Tourism Authority (☞ Visitor Information, *below*) for schedules.

Car Rental

You'll need a valid driver's license to rent a car, and you must meet the minimum age requirements of each rental service (Budget, for example, requires drivers to be over 25; Avis, between the ages of 23 and 70; and Hertz, over 21). A deposit of $500 (or a signed credit-card slip) is required. Rates are between $35 and $65 a day (local agencies generally have lower rates). Insurance is available starting at $10 per day, and all companies offer unlimited mileage. Try to make reservations before arriving, and opt for a four-wheel-drive vehicle if you plan to explore the island's natural sights.

➤ AGENCIES: **Avis** (Kolibristraat 14, Oranjestad, tel. 297/8–28787; Airport, tel. 297/8–25496), **Budget Rent-a-Car** (Kolibristraat 1,

Oranjestad, tel. 297/8–28600 or 800/472–3325), **Dollar Rent-a-Car** (Grendeaweg 15, Oranjestad, tel. 297/8–22783; Airport, tel. 297/8–25651; Manchebo Beach Resort, J. E. Irausquin Blvd. 55, tel. 297/8–26696), **Economy** (Kolibristraat 5, tel. 297/8–25176), **Hedwina Car Rental** (Bubali 93A, Noord, tel. 297/8–76442; Airport, tel. 297/8–30880), **Hertz** (Sabana Blanco 35, near the airport, tel. 297/8–21845; Airport, tel. 297/8–29112), **National** (Tanki Leendert 170, Noord, tel. 297/8–71967; Airport, tel. 297/8–25451), **Thrifty** (Balashi 65, Santa Cruz, tel. 297/8–55300; Airport, tel. 297/8–35335).

Car Travel

The major attractions are fairly easy to find; others you'll happen upon only by sheer luck (or with an Aruban friend). Aside from the major highways, the island's winding roads are poorly marked (though this is slowly changing). International traffic signs and Dutch-style traffic signals (with an extra light for a turning lane) can be misleading if you're not used to them; use extreme caution, especially at intersections, until you grasp the rules of the road. Speed limits are rarely posted but are usually 80 kph (50 mph) in the countryside.

GASOLINE

Gas prices average $1 a liter (roughly ⅓ gallon), which is reasonable by Caribbean standards. Gas stations are plentiful in and near Oranjestad, San Nicolas, and Santa Cruz and near the major high-rise hotels on the western coast. All take cash (U.S. dollars or florins), and most take major credit cards.

PARKING

There aren't any parking meters in downtown Oranjestad, and finding an open spot is very difficult. Try the lot on Calle G. F. Betico Croes (across from the First National Bank), the one on Havenstraat near the Chez Matilde restaurant, or the one on Emanstraat near the water tower. Rates average Afl2 or $1.25 an hour.

Children on Aruba

Kids of all ages love the beach and, therefore, love Aruba. Resorts are increasingly sensitive to families' needs, and many now have extensive children's programs and can arrange for a baby-sitter. On sightseeing days try to **include some activities that will also interest your kids.** If you are renting a car, don't forget to **arrange for a car seat** when you reserve.

FLYING

If your children are two or older, **ask about children's airfares.** As a general rule, infants under two not occupying a seat fly at greatly reduced fares or even for free. When booking, **confirm carry-on allowances** if you're traveling with infants. In general, for babies charged 10% of the adult fare you are allowed one carry-on bag and a collapsible stroller; if the flight is full, the stroller may have to be checked or you may be limited to less.

Experts agree that it's a good idea to use safety seats aloft for children weighing less than 40 pounds. Airlines set their own policies: U.S. carriers usually require that the child be ticketed, even if he or she is young enough to ride free, since the seats must be strapped into regular seats. Do **check your airline's policy about using safety seats during takeoff and landing.** And since safety seats are not allowed just everywhere in the plane, get your seat assignments early.

When reserving, **request children's meals or a freestanding bassinet** if you need them. But note that bulkhead seats, where you must sit to use the bassinet, may lack an overhead bin or storage space on the floor.

FOOD

Even if your youngsters are picky eaters, meals in the Caribbean shouldn't be a problem. Baby food is easy to find, and hamburgers and hot dogs are available at many resorts. Restaurant menus offer pasta and vegetarian dishes, pizza, sandwiches, and ice cream—all of which appeal to kids.

Supermarkets have cereal, snacks, and other packaged goods you'll recognize from home. At outdoor markets a few dollars will buy you enough bananas, mangoes, and other fresh fruit to last your entire vacation.

LODGING

Children are welcome in most Aruban resorts, and those under 12 or 16 can often stay free in their parents' room (be sure to **find out the cutoff age for children's discounts** when booking). Some places have only limited children's activities, however.

PRECAUTIONS

To avoid immigration problems if your child carries a different last name, **bring identification that clarifies the family relationship** (e.g., a birth certificate identifying the parent or a joint passport).

SUPPLIES & EQUIPMENT

Suites at many resorts and even small hotels have hide-a-beds suitable for children sharing a parent's room. High chairs and cribs are also generally available. Supermarkets sell common brands of disposable diapers, baby food, and other necessities. Bookstores and souvenir shops have activity books and toys that kids will enjoy on vacation and back at home.

Cruise Travel

Cruising is a relaxed and convenient way to tour this beautiful part of the world: you get all of the amenities of a luxury hotel and enough activities to guarantee fun, even on rainy days. All your important decisions are made long before you board. Your itinerary is set, and you know the total cost of your vacation beforehand.

Ships usually call at several ports on a single voyage but are at each for only one day. Thus, although you may be exposed to several islands, you don't get much of a feel for any one of them. To get the best deal on a cruise, **consult a cruise-only travel agency.**

➤ CRUISE LINES: **Carnival Cruise Lines** (3655 N.W. 87th Ave., Miami, FL 33178, tel. 305/599–2600 or 800/227–6482), **Celebrity Cruises** (1050 Caribbean Way, Miami, FL 33122), **Commodore/Crown Cruise Line** (4000 Hollywood Blvd., 385-S Tower, Hollywood, FL 33021, tel. 954/967–2100 or 800/832–1122), **Crystal Cruises** (2049 Century Park E, Suite 1400, Los Angeles, CA 90067, tel. 800/446–6620), **Cunard Line** (6100 Blue Lagoon Dr., Suite 400, Miami, FL 33126, tel. 800/221–4770), **Holland America Line** (300 Elliott Ave. W, Seattle, WA 98119, tel. 800/426–0327), **Norwegian Cruise Line** (95 Merrick Way, Coral Gables, FL 33134, tel. 800/327–7030), **Princess Cruises** (10100 Santa Monica Blvd., Los Angeles, CA 90067, tel. 310/553–1770 or 800/774–6237), **Radisson Seven Seas Cruises** (600 Corporate Dr., Suite 410, Fort Lauderdale, FL 33334, tel. 800/333–3333), **Regal Cruises** (300 Regal Cruises Way, Box 1329, Palmetto, FL 34220, tel. 800/270–7245), **Royal Caribbean Cruise Line** (1050 Caribbean Way, Miami, FL 33132, tel. 800/327–6700), **Seabourn Cruise Line** (6100 Blue Lagoon Dr., Suite 400, Miami, FL 33126, tel. 800/929–9391), **Shipping Cruise Services, Ltd.** (75 Valencia Ave., Coral Gables, FL 33134, tel. 800/258–2633), **Star Clippers** (4101 Salzedo St., Coral Gables, FL 33146, tel. 800/442–0551), **Windstar Cruises** (300 Elliott Ave. W, Seattle, WA 98119, tel. 206/281–3535 or 800/258–7245).

➤ ORGANIZATIONS: **Cruise Lines International Association** (CLIA; 500 5th Ave., Suite 1407, New York, NY 10110, tel. 212/921–0066).

Customs & Duties

When shopping, **keep receipts** for all purchases. Upon reentering the country, **be ready to show customs officials what you've bought.** If you feel a duty is incorrect or object to the way your clearance was handled, note the inspector's badge number and ask to see a supervisor. If the problem isn't resolved, write to the appropriate authorities, beginning with the port director at your point of entry.

IN ARUBA

You can bring up to 1 liter of spirits, 3 liters of beer, or 2.25 liters of wine per person, and up to 200 cigarettes or 20 cigars. You don't need to declare the value of gifts or other items, although customs officials may inquire about large items or large quantities of items and charge (at their discretion) an import tax of 7.5% to 22% on items worth more than $230 (Afl350). Meat, birds, and illegal substances are forbidden. You may be asked to provide written verification that plants are free of diseases. If you're traveling with pets, bring a veterinarian's note attesting to their good health.

➤ INFORMATION: **Aruba Customs Office** (tel. 297/8–21800).

IN AUSTRALIA

Australian residents who are 18 or older may bring home $A400 worth of souvenirs and gifts (including jewelry), 250 cigarettes or 250 grams of tobacco, and 1,125 ml of alcohol (including wine, beer, and spirits). Residents under 18 may bring back $A200 worth of goods. Prohibited items include meat products. Seeds, plants, and fruits need to be declared upon arrival.

➤ INFORMATION: **Australian Customs Service** (Regional Director, Box 8, Sydney, NSW 2001, tel. 02/9213–2000, fax 02/9213–4000).

IN CANADA

Canadian residents who have been out of Canada for at least seven days may bring home C$500 worth of goods duty-free. If you've been away less than seven days but more than 48 hours, the duty-free allowance drops to C$200; if your trip lasts 24–48 hours, the allowance is C$50. You may not pool allowances with family members. Goods claimed under the C$500 exemption may follow you by mail; those claimed under the lesser exemptions must accompany you. Alcohol and tobacco products may be included in the seven-day and 48-hour exemptions but not in the 24-hour exemption. If you meet the age requirements of the province or territory through which you reenter Canada, you may bring in, duty-free, 1.14 liters (40 imperial ounces) of wine or liquor or 24 12-ounce cans or bottles of beer or ale. If you are 16 or older you may bring in, duty-free, 200 cigarettes and 50 cigars. Check ahead of time with Revenue Canada or the Department of Agriculture for policies regarding meat products, seeds, plants, and fruits.

You may send an unlimited number of gifts worth up to C$60 each duty-free to Canada. Label the package UNSOLICITED GIFT—VALUE UNDER $60. Alcohol and tobacco are excluded.

➤ **INFORMATION: Revenue Canada** (2265 St. Laurent Blvd. S, Ottawa, Ontario K1G 4K3, tel. 613/993–0534, 800/461–9999 in Canada, fax 613/957–8911, www.ccra-adrc.gc.ca).

IN NEW ZEALAND

Homeward-bound residents 17 or older may bring back $700 worth of souvenirs and gifts. Your duty-free allowance also includes 4.5 liters of wine or beer; one 1,125-ml bottle of spirits; and either 200 cigarettes, 250 grams of tobacco, 50 cigars, or a combination of the three up to 250 grams. Prohibited items include meat products, seeds, plants, and fruits.

➤ **INFORMATION: New Zealand Customs** (Custom House, 50 Anzac Ave., Box 29, Auckland, New Zealand, tel. 09/359–6655, fax 09/359–6732).

IN THE UNITED KINGDOM

If you're a U.K. resident, you may bring home from countries outside the European Union, duty-free, 200 cigarettes or 50 cigars; 1 liter of spirits or 2 liters of fortified or sparkling wine or liqueurs; 2 liters of still table wine; 60 ml of perfume; 250 ml of toilet water; plus £136 worth of other goods, including gifts and souvenirs. Prohibited items include meat products, seeds, plants, and fruits.

➤ **INFORMATION: HM Customs and Excise** (Dorset House, Stamford St., Bromley, Kent BR1 1XX, tel. 020/7202–4227).

IN THE UNITED STATES

U.S. residents who have been out of the country for at least 48 hours and who have not used the $600 allowance or any part of it in the past 30 days may bring home $600 worth of foreign goods duty-free. This allowance, higher than the standard $400 exemption, applies to the two dozen countries in the Caribbean Basin Initiative (CBI). If you visit a CBI country and a non-CBI country, such as Martinique, you may still bring in $600 worth of goods duty-free, but no more than $400 may be from the non-CBI country. If you're returning from the U.S. Virgin Islands (USVI), the duty-free allowance is $1,200. If your travel included the USVI and another country—say, the Dominican Republic— the $1,200 allowance still applies, but at least $600 worth of goods must be from the USVI.

U.S. residents 21 and older may bring back 1 liter of alcohol duty-free. In addition, regardless of your age, you are allowed 200 cigarettes and 100 non-Cuban cigars. Antiques, which the U.S. Customs Service defines as objects more than 100 years old, enter duty-free, as do original works of art done entirely by hand, including paintings, drawings, and sculptures.

You may also send packages home duty-free: up to $200 worth of goods for personal use, with a limit of one parcel per addressee per day (except alcohol or tobacco products or perfume worth more than $5); label the package PERSONAL USE and attach a list of its contents and their retail value. Do not label the package UNSOLICITED GIFT or your duty-free exemption will drop to $100. Mailed items do not affect your duty-free allowance on your return.

➤ **INFORMATION: U.S. Customs Service** (1300 Pennsylvania Ave. NW, Washington, DC 20229, www.customs.gov; inquiries tel. 202/354–1000; complaints c/o Office of Regulations and

Rulings; registration of equipment c/o Resource Management, tel. 202/927–0540).

Electricity

Aruba runs on a 110-volt cycle, the same as in the United States; outlets are usually the two-prong variety. Total blackouts are rare, and most large hotels have backup generators.

Emergencies

DIVERS' ALERT

Don't fly within 24 hours of scuba diving. In an emergency, Air Ambulance, run by Rupert Richard, will fly you to Curaçao at a low altitude if you need to get to a decompression chamber.

➤ **CONTACTS: Air Ambulance:** tel. 297/8–29197. **Ambulance and Fire:** tel. 115. **Hospital: Dr. Horacio Oduber Hospital** (L. G. Smith Blvd., across from Costa Linda Beach Resort and the Alhambra Bazaar and Casino, tel. 297/8–74300). **Pharmacy: Botica Eagle** (L. G. Smith Blvd., near hospital, tel. 297/8–76103). **Police:** tel. 111000.

Health

FOOD & DRINK

As a rule, water is pure and food is wholesome in hotels and local restaurants throughout Aruba, but **be cautious when buying food from street and/or beach vendors.** And just as you would at home, **wash or peel all fruits and vegetables** before eating them. Traveler's diarrhea, caused by consuming contaminated water, unpasteurized milk and milk products, and unrefrigerated food, isn't a big problem—unless it happens to you. So **watch what you eat,** especially at outdoor buffets in the hot sun. Make sure cooked food is hot and cold food has been properly refrigerated.

Mild cases of diarrhea may respond to Imodium (known generically as loperamide) or Pepto-Bismol (not as strong), both of which can be purchased in local pharmacies. Drink plenty of bottled water, which is readily available, to keep from becoming dehydrated. A salt-sugar solution (½ teaspoon salt and 4 tablespoons sugar) per quart of water is a good remedy for rehydrating yourself.

PESTS & OTHER HAZARDS

The major health risk is sunburn or sunstroke. A long-sleeve shirt, a hat, and long pants or a beach wrap are essential on a boat, for midday at the beach, and whenever you go out sightseeing. **Use sunscreen** with an SPF of at least 15—especially if you're fair—and apply it liberally on your nose, ears, and other sensitive and exposed areas. **Make sure the sunscreen is waterproof** if you're engaging in water sports, **limit your sun time** for the first few days, and **drink plenty of liquids,** monitoring intake of caffeine and alcohol, which hasten the dehydration process.

Mosquitoes and flies can be bothersome, so **pack some repellent.** The strong trade winds are a relief in the subtropical climate, but don't hang your bathing suit on a balcony—it will probably blow away. Help Arubans conserve water and energy: turn off air-conditioning when you leave your room, and don't let water run unnecessarily.

SHOTS & MEDICATIONS

No special shots or vaccinations are required for Caribbean destinations.

➤ HEALTH WARNINGS: **National Centers for Disease Control** (CDC; National Center for Infectious Diseases, Division of Quarantine, Traveler's Health Section, 1600 Clifton Rd. NE, M/S E-03, Atlanta, GA 30333, tel. 888/232–3228, fax 888/232–3299, www.cdc.gov).

Holidays

Aruba's official holidays include New Year's Day, Betico Croes' Birthday (politician who aided Aruba's transition to semi-independence; Jan. 25), Carnival Monday (Feb. 26 in 2001 and Feb. 11 in 2002), National Anthem and Flag Day (Mar. 18), Good Friday (Apr. 13 in 2001 and Mar. 29 in 2002), Easter Monday (Apr. 16 in 2001 and Mar. 31 in 2002), Queen's Birthday (Apr. 30), Labor Day (May 1), Ascension Day (May 25 in 2001 and May 9 in 2002), Christmas (Dec. 25–26).

Language, Culture, & Etiquette

Everyone on the island speaks English, but the official language is Dutch. Most locals, however, speak Papiamento—a fascinating, rapid-fire mix of Spanish, Dutch, English, French, and Portuguese as well as African and Indian tongues—in normal conversation.

It's best not to mention to residents how "American" everything is—many have settled here from South America and Europe. Aruba has a separate status with the Kingdom of the Netherlands, allowing it to handle its own aviation, customs, immigration, communications, and other internal matters, but the island does retain strong economic, cultural, and political ties with Holland.

Mail

You can send an airmail letter from Aruba to the United States or Canada (it will take 7–14 days) for AFl2 and a postcard for AFl1.15; a letter to Europe (2–3 weeks) is AFl1.75, a postcard AFl1. Prices to Australia and New Zealand (3–4 weeks) may be slightly higher. When addressing letters to Aruba, don't worry about the lack of "formal" addresses (in some places) or postal codes; the island's postal service knows where to go.

If you need to send a package in a hurry, there are a few options to get the job done. The Federal Express office across from the airport offers overnight service to the United States if you get your package in before 3 PM. Another big courier service is UPS, and there are also several smaller local courier services that provide international deliveries, most of them open weekdays 9–5. Check the local phone book for details.

➤ COURIER SERVICES: **Federal Express** (Browninvest Financial Center, Wayaca 31-A, Oranjestad, tel. 297/9–29039). **UPS** (Rockefellerstraat 3, Oranjestad, tel. 297/8–28646).

Money Matters

CURRENCY

Arubans happily accept U.S. dollars virtually everywhere. That said, there's no real need to exchange money, except for necessary pocket change (for soda machines or pay phones). The official currency is the Aruban florin (AFl), also called the guilder, which is made up of 100 cents. Silver coins come in denominations of 1, 2½, 5, 10, 25, and 50 (the square one) cents. Paper currency comes in denominations of 5, 10, 25, 50, and 100 florins.

At press time exchange rates were AFl1.77 per U.S. dollar for cash, AFl1.79 for traveler's checks, and AFl1.51 per Canadian dollar. Stores, hotels, and restaurants converted at AFl1.80; supermarkets and gas stations at AFl1.75. The Dutch Antillean florin—used on Bonaire and Curaçao—isn't accepted here. Prices quoted throughout this book are in U.S. dollars unless otherwise noted.

ATMS

If you need fast cash, you'll find ATMs that accept international cards (and dispense cash in the local currency) at banks in Oranjestad, at the major malls, and along the roads leading to the hotel strip.

➤ BANKS WITH ATMS: **ABN/Amro Bank** (Caya G. F. Betico Croes 89, Oranjestad, tel. 297/8–21515). **Caribbean Mercantile Bank** (Caya G. F. Betico Croes 5, Oranjestad, tel. 297/8–23118).

CREDIT CARDS & TRAVELER'S CHECKS

Major credit cards are widely accepted at hotels, restaurants, shops, car-rental agencies, and other service providers throughout Aruba. The only places that might not accept them are open-air markets or tiny shops in out-of-the-way villages.

It's smart to **write down (and keep separate) the number of the credit card(s) you're carrying** and the toll-free number to call in case the card is lost or stolen.

Throughout this guide the following abbreviations are used: **AE,** American Express; **D,** Discover; **DC,** Diner's Club; **MC,** Master Card; and **V,** Visa.

Get traveler's checks in small denominations—$20 or $50. Restaurants and most shops will accept them (with ID), and your hotel will cash them for you, though you might get change in local currency. In rural areas and small villages you'll need cash. Lost or stolen checks can usually be replaced within 24 hours. **Buy and pay for your own traveler's checks;** the person who bought the checks must request the refund.

SERVICE CHARGES, TIPPING, & TAXES

Hotels usually add an 11% service charge to the bill and collect a 6% government tax. Restaurants generally include a 10%–15% service charge on the bill; when in doubt, ask. If service isn't included, a 10% tip is standard; if it is included, it's still customary to add something extra, usually small change, at your discretion. Taxi drivers expect a 10%–15% tip, but it isn't mandatory. Porters and bellmen should receive about $2 per bag; chambermaids about $2 a day, but check to see if their tips are included in your bill so you don't overpay. The airport departure tax is a whopping $34.50, but the fee is usually included in your ticket price. Children under two years old fly free and don't pay departure tax. For purchases you'll pay a 6.5% ABB tax (a value-added tax) in all but the duty-free shops.

Packing

Dress on Aruba is generally casual. **Bring loose-fitting clothing made of natural fabrics** to see you through days of heat and humidity. **Pack a beach cover-up,** both to protect yourself from the sun and to provide something to wear to and from your hotel room. Bathing suits and immodest attire are frowned upon off the beach. A sun hat is advisable, but you don't have to pack one—inexpensive straw hats are available everywhere. For shopping and sightseeing, bring walking shorts, jeans, T-shirts, long-sleeve cotton shirts, slacks, and sundresses. Nighttime dress can range from really informal to casually elegant, depending on the establishment. A tie is practically never required, but a jacket may be appropriate in fancy restaurants. You may need a light sweater or jacket for evenings.

In your carry-on luggage, **pack an extra pair of eyeglasses or contact lenses** (but if you forget, there are several eyecare centers in town where you can pick up a spare pair of lenses) and **enough of any medication you take** to last the entire trip. You may also ask your doctor to write a spare prescription using the drug's generic name, since brand names may vary from country to country. In luggage to be checked, **never pack prescription drugs or valuables.** To avoid customs delays, carry medications in their original packaging. And don't forget to carry with you the addresses of offices that handle refunds of lost traveler's checks.

CHECKING LUGGAGE

How many carry-on bags you can bring with you is up to the airline. Most allow two but not always, so make sure that everything you carry aboard will fit under your seat or in the overhead bin, and get to the gate early. Note that if you have a seat at the back of the plane, you'll probably board first, while the overhead bins are still empty.

If you are flying internationally, note that baggage allowances may be determined not by piece but by weight—generally 88 pounds (40 kilograms) in first class, 66 pounds (30 kilograms) in business class, and 44 pounds (20 kilograms) in economy.

Airline liability for baggage is limited to $1,250 per person on flights within the United States. On international flights it amounts to $9.07 per pound or $20 per kilogram for checked baggage (roughly $640 per 70-pound bag) and $400 per passenger for unchecked baggage. You can buy additional coverage at check-in for about $10 per $1,000 of coverage, but it excludes a rather extensive list of items, shown on your airline ticket.

Before departure **itemize your bags' contents** and their worth, and label the bags with your name, address, and phone number. (If you use your home address, cover it so potential thieves can't see it readily.) Inside each bag **pack a copy of your itinerary.** At check-in **make sure that each bag is correctly tagged** with the destination airport's three-letter code. If your bags arrive damaged or fail to arrive at all, file a written report with the airline before leaving the airport.

Passports

When traveling internationally, **carry your passport even if you don't need one** (it's always the best form of ID) and **make two photocopies of the data page** (one for someone at home and another for you, carried separately from your passport). If you lose your passport, promptly call the nearest embassy or consulate and the local police.

ENTERING ARUBA

U.S. and Canadian citizens need a valid passport or a birth certificate with a raised seal and a government-issued photo ID. Visitors from the member countries of the European Union must also carry their European Union Travel Card, as well as a passport. All other nationalities must have a valid passport.

PASSPORT OFFICES

The best time to apply for a passport or to renew is in fall and winter. Before any trip check your passport's expiration date and, if necessary, renew it as soon as possible.

➤ **AUSTRALIAN CITIZENS: Australian Passport Office** (tel. 131–232, www.dfat.gov.au/passports).

➤ **CANADIAN CITIZENS: Passport Office (**tel. 819/994–3500 or 800/567–6868, www.dfait-maeci.gc.ca/passport).

➤ **NEW ZEALAND CITIZENS: New Zealand Passport Office** (tel. 04/494–0700, www.passports.govt.nz).

➤ **U.K. CITIZENS: London Passport Office** (tel. 0990/210–410) for fees and documentation requirements and for an emergency passport.

➤ **U.S. CITIZENS: National Passport Information Center** (tel. 900/225–5674; calls are 35¢ per minute for automated service, $1.05 per minute for operator service).

Rest Rooms

Outside of Oranjestad, the only public rest rooms you'll find will be in one of the few restaurants that dot the countryside.

Safety

Arubans are very friendly, so you needn't be afraid to stop and ask anyone for directions. It's a relatively safe island, but common-sense rules still apply. Lock your rental car when you leave it, and leave valuables in your hotel safe. Don't leave bags unattended in the airport, on the beach, or on tour transports.

Shopping

For many, shopping on Aruba means duty-free bargains on jewelry, designer clothing, china, crystal, and other luxury goods from around the world. At the Aruba Trading Company in the airport departure hall (on the left, near U.S. immigration), you'll find a complete selection of duty-free liquors, tobacco, and perfumes. For others, shopping means buying locally produced crafts and works of art.

Bargaining isn't expected in shops, but at open-air markets and with street vendors it may be acceptable. Keep in mind, however, that selling handicrafts or home-grown produce may be a local's only livelihood. When bargaining, consider the amount of work or effort involved and the item's value to you. Vendors don't set artificially high prices and then expect to bargain; they bargain so you'll buy from them instead of their neighbor.

Taxis

There's a dispatch office at the airport; you can also flag down taxis on the street (look for license plates with a "TX" tag). Rates are fixed (i.e., there are no meters; the rates are set by the government and displayed on a chart), though you and the driver should agree on the fare before your ride begins. Add $1 to the fare after midnight and $1–$3 on Sunday and holidays. An hour-long island tour costs about $30, with up to four people. Rides into town from Eagle Beach run about $5; from Palm Beach, about $8.

➤ Taxi Service: **Airport Taxi Dispatch** (tel. 297/8–22116).

Telephones

To call Aruba direct from the United States, dial 011–297–8, followed by the five-digit number in Aruba. (To call from elsewhere abroad, substitute 011 with the country of origin's international access code.) International, direct, and operator-assisted calls from Aruba are possible to all countries in the world via hotel operators or from the Government Long Distance Telephone, Telegraph, and Radio Office (SETAR), in the post-office building in Oranjestad. When making calls on Aruba, simply dial the five-digit number. AT&T customers can dial 800–8000 from special phones at the cruise dock and in the airport's arrival and departure halls. From other phones dial 121 to contact the SETAR International Operator to place a collect or AT&T calling card call. Local calls from pay phones, which accept both local currency and phone cards, cost 25¢. Business travelers or vacationers who need to be in regular contact with their families at home can rent an international cell phone from the concierge in most hotels or at some local electronics stores.

Tours & Packages

Because everything is prearranged on a prepackaged tour or independent vacation, you'll spend less time planning—and often get it all at a good price.

BOOKING WITH AN AGENT

Travel agents are excellent resources. But it's a good idea to collect brochures from several agencies, as some agents' suggestions may be influenced by relationships with tour and package firms that reward them for volume sales. If you have a special interest, **find an agent with expertise in that area.** The American Society of Travel Agents (ASTA; ☞ Travel Agencies, *below*) has a database of specialists worldwide.

Make sure your travel agent knows the accommodations and other services of the place being recommended. Ask about the hotel's location, room size, beds, and whether it has a pool, room service, or programs for children, if you care about these. Has your agent been there in person or sent others whom you can contact?

Do some homework on your own, too: local tourism boards can provide information about lesser-known and small-niche operators, some of which may sell only direct.

BUYER BEWARE

Each year consumers are stranded or lose their money when tour operators—even large ones with excellent reputations—go out of business. So **check out the operator.** Ask several travel agents about its reputation and try to **book with a company that has a consumer-protection program.** (Look for information in the company's brochure.) In the United States members of the

National Tour Association (NTA) and the United States Tour Operators Association (USTOA) are required to set aside funds to cover your payments and travel arrangements in the event that the company defaults. It's also a good idea to choose a company that participates in ASTA's Tour Operator Program (TOP); ASTA will act as mediator in any disputes between you and your tour operator.

Remember that the more your package or tour includes the better you can predict the ultimate cost of your vacation. Make sure you know exactly what is covered and **beware of hidden costs.** Are taxes, tips, and transfers included? Entertainment and excursions? These can add up.

➤ TOUR-OPERATOR RECOMMENDATIONS: **American Society of Travel Agents** (Travel Agencies, *below*). **National Tour Association** (NTA; 546 E. Main St., Lexington, KY 40508, tel. 606/226–4444 or 800/682–8886, www.ntaonline.com). **United States Tour Operators Association** (USTOA; 342 Madison Ave., Suite 1522, New York, NY 10173, tel. 212/599–6599 or 800/468–7862, fax 212/599–6744, www.ustoa.com).

ISLAND TOURS

If you try a cruise around the island, know that the choppy waters are stirred up by trade winds and that catamarans are much smoother than monohulls. Sucking on a peppermint or lemon candy may help a queasy stomach; avoid going with an empty or overly full stomach. Moonlight cruises cost about $25 per person. There are also a variety of snorkeling, dinner and dancing, and sunset party cruises to choose from, priced from $25 to $60 per person. Many of the smaller operators work out of their homes; they often offer to pick you up (and drop you off) at your hotel or meet you at particular hotel pier.

Explore an underwater reef teeming with marine life without getting wet. Atlantis Submarines operates a 20-m (65-ft) air-conditioned sub that takes 48 passengers 29–46 m (95–150 ft) below the surface along Barcadera Reef. The two-hour trip (including boat transfer to the submarine platform and 50-minute plunge) costs $72. Make reservations one day in advance. Another option is the *Seaworld Explorer*, a semisubmersible that allows you to sit and view Aruba's marine habitat from 2 m (6 ft) below the surface. The cost is $35 for a 1½-hour tour.

You can see the main sights in one day, but set aside two days to really meander. Guided tours are your best option if you have only a short time. Aruba's Transfer Tour & Taxi C.A. takes you to the main sights on personalized tours that cost $30 per hour.

De Palm Tours has a near monopoly on Aruban sightseeing; you can make reservations through its general office or at hotel tour-desk branches. The company's basic 3½-hour tour hits the highlights. Wear tennis or hiking shoes, and bring a lightweight jacket or wrap (the air-conditioned bus gets cold). It begins at 9:30 AM, picks you up in your hotel lobby, and costs $22.50 per person. A full-day Jeep Adventure tour ($59.50 per person) takes you to sights that would be difficult for you to find on your own. Bring a bandanna to cover your mouth; the ride on rocky dirt roads can get dusty. De Palm also offers full-day tours of Curaçao ($219; every Friday). Prices include round-trip airfare, transfers, sightseeing, and lunch; there's free time for shopping.

Romantic horse-drawn-carriage rides through the city streets of Oranjestad run $30 for a 30-minute tour; hours of operation are 7 PM–11 PM, and carriages depart from the clock tower at the Royal Plaza Mall.

➤ BOAT TOUR OPERATORS: **Atlantis Submarines** (Seaport Village Marina, tel. 297/8–36090). **De Palm Tours** (L. G. Smith Blvd. 142, Oranjestad, tel. 297/8–24400 or 800/766–6016). **Jolly Pirates** (tel. 297/8–37355). **Pelican Watersports** (J. E. Irausquin Blvd. 230, Oranjestad, tel. 297/8–72302). **Red Sail Sports** (Seaport Village Mall, L. G. Smith Blvd. 82, Oranjestad, tel. 297/8–61603 or 877/733–7245 in the U.S.). **Seaworld Explorer** (tel. 297/8–62416).

➤ ORIENTATION TOUR OPERATORS: **Aruba's Transfer Tour & Taxi C.A.** (Pos Abao 41, Oranjestad, tel. 297/8–22116). **De Palm Tours** (L. G. Smith Blvd. 142, Oranjestad, tel. 297/8–24400 or 800/766–6016).

Travel Agencies

A good travel agent puts your needs first. Look for an agency that has been in business at least five years, emphasizes customer service, and has someone on staff who specializes in your destination. In addition, **make sure the agency belongs to a professional trade organization.** The American Society of Travel Agents (ASTA), with 27,000 agents in some 170 countries, is the largest and most influential in the field. Operating under the motto "Integrity in Travel," it maintains and enforces a strict code of ethics and will step in to help mediate any agent-client disputes if necessary. ASTA also maintains a Web site that includes a directory of agents. (If a travel agency is also acting as your tour operator, *see* Buyer Beware *in* Tours & Packages, *above*.)

➤ LOCAL AGENT REFERRALS: **American Society of Travel Agents** (ASTA; tel. 800/965–2782 24-hr hot line, fax 703/684–8319, www.astanet.com). **Association of British Travel Agents** (68–71 Newman St., London W1P 4AH, tel. 020/7637–2444, fax 020/7637–0713, www.abtanet.com). **Association of Canadian Travel Agents** (1729 Bank St., Suite 201, Ottawa, Ontario K1V 7Z5, tel. 613/521–0474, fax 613/521–0805). **Australian Federation of Travel Agents** (Level 3, 309 Pitt St., Sydney 2000, tel. 02/9264–3299, fax 02/9264–1085, www.afta.com.au). **Travel Agents' Association of New Zealand** (Box 1888, Wellington 10033, tel. 04/499–0104, fax 04/499–0827).

Time

Aruba is in the Atlantic Standard Time zone, which is one hour later than Eastern Standard Time or four hours earlier than Greenwich mean time. During Daylight Saving Time, between April and October, Atlantic Standard is the same time as Eastern Daylight Time.

Visitor Information

Before leaving home, contact the Aruba Tourism Authority at one of its many offices. The Caribbean Tourism Organization (CTO) is another good resource. On Aruba the tourist office has free brochures and information officers who are ready to answer any questions you may have, weekdays 7:30–4:30.

➤ ARUBA INFORMATION: **Aruba Tourism Authority** (tel. 800/862–7822, www.arubatourism.com; L. G. Smith Blvd. 172, Eagle Beach, Aruba, tel. 297/8–23777; 1 Financial Plaza, Suite 136, Fort Lauderdale, FL 33394, tel. 954/767–6477; 3455 Peach Tree Rd. NE, Suite 500, Atlanta, GA 30326, tel. 404/892–7822; 5901 N. Cicero, Suite 301, Chicago, IL, 60646, tel. 773/202–5054; 1000 Harbor Blvd., Ground Level, Weehawken, NJ 07087, tel. 201/330–0800; 12707 North Freeway, Suite 138, Houston, TX 77060-1234, tel. 281/872–7822; Business Centre 5875, Suite 201, Hwy. 7, Vaughan, Ontario, L4L 8Z7, tel. 905/264–3434).

➤ CARIBBEAN-WIDE INFORMATION: **CTO** (80 Broad St., New York, NY 10004, tel. 212/635–9530; Vigilant House, 120 Wilton Rd., London SW1V 1JZ, tel. 020/7233–8382).

➤ U.S. GOVERNMENT ADVISORIES: **U.S. Department of State** (Overseas Citizens Services Office, Room 4811 N.S., 2201 C St. NW, Washington, DC 20520, tel. 202/647–5225 for interactive hot line, 301/946–4400 computer bulletin board, fax 202/647–3000 interactive hot line); **enclose a self-addressed, stamped business-size envelope.**

Web Sites

Do check out the World Wide Web when you're planning. You'll find everything from up-to-date weather forecasts to virtual tours of famous cities. Fodor's Web site, www.fodors.com, is a great place to start your on-line travels.

For information on the Caribbean, visit one of the following: www.caribtourism.com (the CTO's official site, with many island-specific links); www.caribbeanchannel.com (with information presented both thematically and by island); www.caribbeantravel.com (the official Caribbean Hotel Association site); www.caribbeancyberspace.com (for general information and good links); www.caribbeannewspapers.com (with links to newspapers published throughout the Caribbean); www.caribinfo.com (with a directory of Web sites based in or related to the Caribbean and links to local phone directories); www2.prestel.co.uk/caribbean (with aviation routes and schedules as well as links to all airlines that serve the region); www.cruising.org (the Cruise Lines International Association's site, with many ship profiles); www.cananews.com and www.cweek.com (for Caribbean news).

When to Go

Aruba's high season is traditionally winter—from December 15 to April 14—when northern weather is at its worst. During this season you're guaranteed the most entertainment at resorts and the most people with whom to enjoy it. It's also the most fashionable, the most expensive, and the most popular time to visit—and most hotels are heavily booked. You must make reservations at least two or three months in advance for the very best places. Hotel prices drop 20%–40% after April 15; cruise prices also fall.

➤ FORECASTS: **Weather Channel Connection** (tel. 900/932–8437), 95¢ per minute from a Touch-Tone phone.

INDEX

FODOR'S POCKET ARUBA

EDITOR: Laura M. Kidder

EDITORIAL CONTRIBUTORS: Karen W. Bressler and Elise Rosen

EDITORIAL PRODUCTION: Rebecca Zeiler Wintle

MAPS: David Lindroth, *cartographer*; Bob Blake and Rebecca Baer, *map editors*

DESIGN: Fabrizio La Rocca, *creative director*; Tigist Getachew, *art director*

PRODUCTION/MANUFACTURING: Robert B. Shields

COVER PHOTOGRAPH: Darrell Jones/AllStock/PictureQuest

COPYRIGHT

First Edition

ISBN 0-679-00775-X

ISSN 1098-2663

IMPORTANT TIP

Although all prices, opening times, and other details in this book are based on information supplied to us at press time, changes occur all the time in the travel world, and Fodor's cannot accept responsibility for facts that become outdated or for inadvertent errors or omissions. So **always confirm information when it matters**, especially if you're making a detour to visit a specific place.

SPECIAL SALES

Fodor's Travel Publications are available at special discounts for bulk purchases for sales promotions or premiums. Special editions, including personalized covers, excerpts of existing guides, and corporate imprints, can be created in large quantities for special needs. For more information, contact your local bookseller or write to Special Markets, Fodor's Travel Publications, 280 Park Avenue, New York, NY 10017. Inquiries from Canada should be directed to your local Canadian bookseller or sent to Random House of Canada, Ltd., Marketing Department, 2775 Matheson Boulevard East, Mississauga, Ontario L4W 4P7. Inquiries from the United Kingdom should be sent to Fodor's Travel Publications, 20 Vauxhall Bridge Road, London SW1V 2SA, England.

PRINTED IN THE UNITED STATES OF AMERICA

10 9 8 7 6 5 4 3 2 1